Shut Up!

7 Simple Steps to Master Your Negative

Self-Talk, Remove Anxiety Symptoms,
Stop Beating Yourself up, Then Take Back
Power, and Build Good Habits

Mike Nichols

Table of Contents

Introduction

"Accepting you have the ability to create change, then allows you to seek change, which in turn allows you to make change" – *Mike Nichols*

*T*he human mind is a wonderful thing.

Our minds allow us to imagine, explore, and understand the world around us. What we think and believe shapes who we are and it also shapes the world around us.

But what happens to our perceptions of the world if our mind actively tries to play tricks on us? What if what you assumed about your mind was wrong?

Oftentimes, our perceptions are colored by our personal biases and judgments, even more so by our inner voice. If you're reading this book, chances are that your inner voice hasn't been treating you well.

I'd go as far as to say the little voice at the back of your mind has probably been sprouting some pretty mean things and attacking your self-confidence.

Well, the title of this book is *Shut Up! 7 Simple Steps to Master Your Negative Self-Talk, Remove Anxiety Symptoms, Stop Beating Yourself up, Then Take Back Power, and Build Good Habits*, and that's exactly what I intend to help you do.

It is time for your inner voice to shut up and listen to you and what you want. It is time that you take over your inner monologue and start turning that negative self-talk into positive self-talk.

If you're here, you've reached a point in your life where you feel ready for change. You want a solution to whatever problems you've been facing. You want to be understood.

Up until this point, you may have faced numerous challenges, and while those experiences have influenced your life and perceptions, they do not **DEFINE** you.

In this book, I am going to introduce you to powerful insights on the inner workings of your negative self-talk and then show you how to flip that negativity on its head. I will set achievable exercises that you can practice at the end of each chapter. These exercises are aimed at helping you develop your understanding and self-confidence.

You will learn how to implement positive self-talk and minimize the effects of negative self-talk.

The Jeet Kune Do philosophy, founded by Bruce Lee, advocates for focusing on what is useful and getting rid of the unnecessary. While this principle is aimed at martial arts, I think the same can be said about self-growth and development.

I am of the opinion that the things in your life should serve you and your interests. This includes your inner voice and perspective. Everything in your life should be pushing you further in life and closer to your goals.

If something in your life is holding you down or holding you back, get rid of it.

Now, adopting a new mindset and cutting the fat from your life doesn't happen overnight. It isn't easy either. It's going to take work, and you're going to have to put in that work.

I know firsthand how hard it can be to implement change. I used to be shy and introverted; I lacked confidence. However, over time, I learned about the impact my perceptions had on my life and my environment. I took personal development courses, I read books on the topic of self-confidence and inner growth, and I practiced.

I taught myself how to think differently and how to shift my mindset to fit the outcomes that I wanted.

I have over 10 years of experience in helping people understand and overcome negative self-talk. I've worked with people in sports, business, and in life, so let me help you.

If you want to learn more about self-talk and how it affects your life, then this book is for you.

I know that with the right mindset—and equipped with the right tools—you can accomplish anything.

Welcome to the first day of the rest of your life!

Chapter Outline

Chapter 1, titled "Your Powerful Mind," is aimed at raising awareness of the power of your mind and how your perceptions of the world might not be in line with reality. This chapter looks at how your brain processes information and makes decisions. It also focuses on your mind's natural defenses. Lastly, this chapter ends with an exercise focused on mindful breathing.

Chapter 2 discusses the importance of living in the now and being fully present. It looks at the importance of making peace with past experiences and moving on from them. The aim here is to learn from your past and move beyond it. It also looks at the importance of accepting your reality and the benefits of practicing mindfulness.

Chapter 3 addresses the issue of self-talk. In this chapter, I discuss positive and negative self-talk and the effects both have on your perceptions of the world and your well-being. I also look at imposter syndrome and the different kinds of imposter syndrome that you could experience. Lastly, I introduce the concept of submodalities and how it works with negative self-talk.

Chapter 4 focuses on the importance of setting realistic expectations. It discusses the misalignment between expectations and reality and the effects of this on your growth and development. It then goes on to discuss how to set realistic expectations in order to avoid disappointment. Lastly, this chapter ends with an exercise aimed at identifying and dealing with negativity.

Chapter 5 takes a deep dive into your personal relationships. These include friends, family, colleagues, and social media connections. This chapter discusses the impact your personal relationships have on your perceptions of the world and on your thinking. It looks at issues like toxic relationships and how to recognize whether a relationship is healthy or not. This chapter ends with an exercise focused on expanding your awareness to your surroundings and viewing your environment without passing judgment.

Chapter 6 focuses on helping you fully understand, appreciate, and take ownership of your thoughts and emotions. It is also aimed at helping you realize that you have complete power over your thoughts and perceptions.

Chapter 7 urges you to take action and use the tools and information in the previous chapters to improve your life. It is time to practice what I've preached and begin implementing actionable changes to your life.

How to Use This Guide

This guide will take you through seven steps that are aimed at raising your self-awareness and your awareness about your surroundings. Each chapter concludes with an exercise aimed at helping you practice mindfulness and positive self-talk.

These exercises are focused on helping you build up the mental muscle needed to succeed.

Throughout these pages, you will discover how to create good habits that will help you feel in control of your life and your future.

I have to warn you though—as with everything, building healthy mental mindsets and habits takes time and practice. It isn't something that happens overnight. Be patient with yourself, and don't forget to give yourself some grace.

Now, are you ready to start taking action to succeed? Let's go!

Chapter 1:

Your Powerful Mind

Our minds are powerful things. They affect our perception of the world and of ourselves in ways that we cannot imagine.

Often, our perception of things is heavily affected by our own personal biases, fears, hopes, and aspirations. In the introduction, we briefly touched on individual fears and how our inner voices can reflect those fears.

One of the main functions of our minds is to protect us from making mistakes and from harming ourselves. How our minds protect us depends on our perception of what we fear and how much we fear.

But just how are our minds able to perceive the world around us? What affects our perceptions? Do our perceptions affect the way we think and act?

This chapter aims to answer these questions and discusses how our minds process information. The aim here is to better understand how our minds work. This chapter focuses on raising awareness of the power of the mind and how our perceptions of the world can be warped by our internal fears and biases.

First, this chapter looks at how our brains process information. We then go on to discuss the methods our minds use to protect us against the things we fear.

Given the prevalence of social media in our everyday lives, I thought it would be important to look at how this affects our perceptions as well.

I've also included a fun little anecdote called "The Actress and I."

Lastly, I leave you with a coaching action which discusses the importance of mindfulness and gives you a few tips on how to gain an awareness of your physical self.

How Your Brain Processes Information

Have you ever wondered how your brain processes the information around you? How does it seem to make sense of almost everything, from the sounds of cars outside to the words in this book? A simple glance to the paper, and suddenly you've comprehended all the information these words hold.

That's amazing!

How do our brains do it? Are there limits to what our brains can perceive and understand? If so, just how much of reality are we missing out on?

There are millions of questions we could ask about our brain's capabilities and limitations. If you're anything like me, it is very tempting to go slipping down a rabbit hole and going on an endless Google stream trying to find answers, but that's not why we're here.

This section aims to help you understand how your brain processes information. Understanding how your brain processes information and how this affects your perception of the world is a great starting point to addressing maladaptive thinking and a negative internal narrative.

The thinking here is that if you understand how your brain processes information, you'd better be able to understand how and why you perceive things the way you do. This could also help you identify things that trigger your negative narrator or any of your fears.

Once you're able to identify your triggers and understand how your mind works, you should better be able to handle and react to those triggers.

Now, understanding how the human brain works is complicated. There are extremely qualified scientists out there who are still trying to figure it out. To make things simpler, I'll be going over the basics.

Think about your brain as a supercomputer—a self-learning computer if you will. It reacts differently depending on which buttons are pressed, and it adjusts how it reacts the more it gets interacted with.

The brain is a complex machine. It absorbs all of the "raw data" from the outside world and converts this data into manageable, bite-sized chunks that are easier for us to understand. The raw data can be converted into thoughts, perceptions, and memories (Pappas, 2016).

How does it do this?

Well, the brain consists of numerous structures, all of which are connected by neural pathways. The structures I'll be focusing on are the cortex—which is the part responsible for complex thinking—and the subcortex, which is the part directly linked to the cortex (Pappas, 2016).

There are numerous theories that explain how the brain processes information. I'll be simplifying this process into three steps, namely, input, storage, and output.

The first step, input, occurs when the brain is exposed to stimuli. The brain then analyzes and evaluates this information. For example, you might hear a sound, and your brain will evaluate that sound and determine that music is playing. Whether you remember the music or not is determined by your personal preferences.

The second step is storage. As the name implies, storage occurs when the brain retains information that you consider important. Our brains also add this information to our mental schema and encodes it. A downside of this is that if the information is not reinforced, we will forget it over time.

For example, when studying for an exam, we are often forced to retain large amounts of information. However, once the exam is over, most of the information is lost because we are no longer studying it, or we no longer consider it important.

The last step is called output. The output occurs once the brain decides what it wants to do with the information and how to react to a stimulus. Going back to the music example, if you hear a familiar song, you might decide to dance and sing along. This could be your brain deciding on an output/reaction based on your personal preferences.

Being able to process information allows us to make decisions on how to react to the information. When making decisions, the human brain uses two processes: the reactive system and the reflective system.

The Reactive System

At its core, the reactive decision-making system is based on intuition. This kind of decision making kicks in during times of stress or pressure where one needs to make a decision quickly (Gladwell, 2005). It is closely linked to our innate fight-or-flight responses where an action is required but we lack the time to properly consider the consequences of that action.

We've all heard about and experienced "gut feelings" and did what "felt right" without having a proper explanation or reason behind it. This is called intuitive-based decision making.

The Reflective System

The quickest route toward solving a problem or making a decision might not always be the best route. When faced with complex situations, it is sometimes better to think things through by analyzing the available information and figure out the best way to handle it. This is where the reflective decision-making system comes into play.

The reflective decision-making system operates on the opposite spectrum of the reactive system. Instead of making decisions based on impulse, reflective decision making considers all aspects of the situation including emotional responses (Lieberman, 2003).

Emotional responses can often make it difficult for people to process information rationally (Lieberman, 2003). Therefore, it's very important to consider the effects emotions can have on people and the situation surrounding it before making a decision.

Reflective decision making is more thoughtful and considerate than reactive decision making.

Fight-or-Flight Response

Your mind is powerful, and one of its key functions is to ensure that you are protected from danger. However, danger is a relative concept. What you find dangerous, another might find fun. A good example of this is extreme sports and activities such as skydiving or river rafting.

One of the ways that your minds protect us from perceived danger is via our "fight-or-flight" response. Our fight-or-flight response is both physiological and psychological (Cherry, 2019). It's purpose is to prepare the body to react to the perceived danger.

But what happens during a fight-or-flight response? How does it affect our psychology and physiology?.

The Physical and Psychological Effects of the Fight-or-Flight Response

When exposed to an acute stressor our body's sympathetic nervous system is activated. The perceived threat/stressor can be either physical or psychological. For example, it could be triggered by a barking dog or having to prepare a presentation in front of a large group.

The sympathetic nervous system activates our adrenal glands which triggers the release of catecholamines (this includes adrenaline and noradrenaline). This causes an increased heart rate, breathing, and blood pressure (Cherry, 2019). Your entire body tenses up and gets ready for action. This action could be either to fight or flee (flight), depending on your perceived level of fear and danger.

Additional physical fight-or-flight responses include:

- Pale or flushed skin: Your body will reduce blood flow to the surface areas of your body while increasing the flow to your muscles, brain, arms, and legs. This causes pale or flushed skin as blood rushes to your brain and away from your skin.

- Dilated pupils: In order to increase your awareness of the situation and your surroundings, your eyes will dilate. This increases the amount of light that enters your eyes and results in improved vision.

- Shivering: As your body tenses and prepares for action, you will find yourself shivering or trembling in response.

A psychological response to having your fight-or-flight response triggered is experiencing either memory loss or a heightened memory of the experience. Your mind might also alter the specific memory so that it feels less traumatic or denies the experience entirely.

Another trigger for our fight-or-flight response is through phobias. Phobias are a good example of a perceived threat that might not be real. For example, a person with a fear of heights might falsely trigger their fight-or-flight response while on the top floor of a skyscraper. If the response becomes too intense, it could cause a panic attack.

By learning more about our body's natural responses to stress, we are able to explore alternative ways to deal with that stress. This is especially useful if your natural reaction to stress is negative or debilitating, such as a panic attack or memory loss.

How the Mind Protects Itself From Stress or Trauma

Our minds have numerous ways to protect itself from stressors and trauma. However, not all of them are helpful or productive. Many of the methods that our minds use to protect us from trauma can often be quite debilitating or contribute toward our stress.

Being aware of how your mind deals with stress and trauma is the first step toward learning how to deal with your stressors in a healthier way.

Below are a few methods that our minds use to protect itself from stress:

Denial

A common method that our minds use to protect itself from a stressful or traumatic experience is to deny that it ever happened in the first place. Your mind might do this by either forcefully forgetting the experience or altering your memory of it.

These actions are aimed at protecting you from the emotional and psychological distress that these memories and experiences might trigger. By denying that the event happened, you are pardoned from having to deal with the consequences of the event.

Depending on the perceived severity of the trauma or stressors, denial could lead to a more serious response such as dissociation.

Dissociation occurs when the brain experiences excessive trauma and responses by "removing" itself from the situation that might be causing the trauma (Tull, 2019). This could lead to feeling emotionally and mentally detached, experiencing memory loss, and lacking a sense of self (Tull, 2019).

Avoidance

When faced with the possibility of a stressful situation, your brain might decide to avoid it instead of having to experience it. The simplest example of this is procrastination. We've all procrastinated; whether that was procrastinating on studying for a test or starting an assignment or even taking a shower, there's never been a moment where it hasn't occurred.

Oftentimes, the reason we procrastinate is because we're avoiding the stress that comes along with doing the task. Doing a presentation is stressful, having to do an assignment is stressful, and depending on our mental well-being, taking a shower can be stressful.

In order to protect ourselves from the perceived stress, our minds will avoid the situation entirely. This avoidance can be either conscious or unconscious.

One of the best ways to combat this avoidance is to figure out the cause of it. Are you procrastinating on studying because you're afraid of failure? Are you avoiding applying for a job because you fear rejection?

Once you figure out the cause of your avoidance, it helps you find healthier ways of dealing with it.

Shifting the Blame

We are responsible for our actions and reactions to things—with that responsibility comes accountability.

If we refuse to study for an important test and we fail that test, that's on us. It's truly our fault, but coming to terms with our own shortcomings and failures can be stressful. It can also be quite traumatic.

Facing our flaws and shortcomings can cause us to question our sense of self. Are our flaws preventing us from living up to both external and internal expectations?

These questions alone are enough to cause some people to experience feelings of stress.

One of the ways our minds protects us from this stress is by shifting the blame. When something bad happens, whether that's failing a test or being fired, it is only natural for us to look for something or someone to blame.

Of course it wasn't our fault we failed the test. It is the teacher's fault for making the test too difficult.

In doing so, we twist our reality in order to protect our self-esteem and guard us against our fear of failure (Cherry, 2019).

Social Media Mentality

Social media has infiltrated every aspect of our lives. There are more social media apps and platforms than I have fingers and toes, and chances are, you're using more than one of them.

Now, I want to make one thing clear: Social media isn't inherently bad. In fact, in the age of the Coronavirus, social media and technology has allowed us to stay close to our loved ones during intense lockdown restrictions and social distancing.

The introduction of social media has also created thousands, if not millions, of jobs that have boosted the economy. Social media created new career streams and kick-started numerous careers.

My point is that social media has done us all a lot of good, and we shouldn't be so quick to dismiss the good it has done.

That being said, as with most things, the effect social media has toward you depends on how you use it. Social media can be quite addictive. I'm pretty sure I'm not the only one who lost hours on TikTok and Facebook, scrolling through feeds and videos.

While social media hasn't been around long enough for analysts to accurately study the long-term effects it has on our emotional and mental well-being, a few effects have emerged.

However, there are still a few negative effects of misusing social media platforms.

Increased Feelings of Inadequacy

Social media has quickly introduced new ways to measure our popularity. On Facebook, popularity is measured in likes, comments, and shares. These three aspects have carried on over to Snapchat, Instagram, and Twitter.

With increased social media engagement, it can become easy to begin valuing our own self-worth based on how many likes our pictures and posts get. This kind of thinking is a slippery slope.

Equating your worth to the amount of likes you get can really harm your self-confidence. It can make you feel inadequate and can have you begin comparing yourself to others.

Social media makes comparison ridiculously easy.

People are constantly posting about their lives. This could be showing off their holiday trips, their outings or dates, and whatever aspects of their lives that they choose to show.

Comparing the highlight reel of others to your own life can make you feel as though you can't measure up to the lives of others. It can make you feel as though the things that you've achieved are meaningless.

Negative Body Image

Stemming from the point mentioned above, comparisons on social media could also lead to having a negative body image.

One of the staples of social media is filters. These range from cartoonish filters to "beauty" filters and everything in between. Filters have improved so much that it has become difficult to distinguish the difference between what's real and what's not.

If you look at popular Instagram accounts, you'll find tons of beautiful people with perfect bodies wearing designer clothes, and this can contribute to your own insecurities.

You might compare your body and see your flaws and then compare them to the perceived perfection of others, but how much of what you see is real? Many of the photos that you see online have been altered by Photoshop and filters.

The "perfection" that you see online might be illusions.

While body image issues are common, it is important to remember that everyone is human. We all have flaws and imperfections, and there is nothing wrong with that. It is also important to remember that social media influencers allow you to see what they want you to see. You are never getting the full picture.

Increased Depression and Anxiety

Social media can be quite addictive. It is easy to get lost on YouTube or Instagram; however, spending too much time on these platforms can have a negative impact on your mental health (Stegner, 2020).

This is often because of our innate habit of comparing ourselves and our lives to others. Linking to the two points previously mentioned, constantly feeling inadequate on social media could lead to feelings of depression and anxiety.

Feeling that you'll never measure up or be good enough can cause you to lack confidence in yourself.

While there is nothing inherently wrong with social media, I would advise that you use these platforms mindfully and with caution.

Cyberbullying

Before the invention of the Internet, bullying took place with face-to-face interactions—usually at schools or places of work. However, social media and the Internet has added another platform to the mix (Stegner, 2020).

Social media has made it easier for people to bully others online. After all, it allows you to remain as anonymous as you want and hide behind a screen. All it takes are a few typed words to ruin someone's day. The anonymity also removes any sense of responsibility and consequences for the bullying. If no one knows who you are, how can they hold you accountable for what you've said?

Online attacks can deeply hurt people, and unlike in-person bullying, there is rarely an easy escape, especially if you're always online.

The Actress and I

Amelia is an up-and-coming actress. Before meeting her a few weeks ago, I'd seen her in a few indie films. It was clear from her social media presence that her fans adored her. To an outsider like me, it seemed as though she was on the cusp of greatness. She seemed bubbly, confident, and cheerful.

How wrong that impression was.

The Amelia I met was deeply insecure and lacked the confidence she projected online and in her films. She questioned everything she did and didn't really trust her instincts.

It took a while before she was ready to confront her problems and herself. It was difficult for her to be honest with herself. Like most people, she was living in denial.

We spent weeks going through various exercises during our coaching sessions. We spoke about her negative self-talk and tried figuring out where it came from. After, we worked on building an action plan and discussed how to best execute that plan.

All of that hard work led up to this moment.

Amelia stood stiff, her hand trembling as it reached for the phone. She was nervous. If I was being honest with myself, so was I. I smiled at her encouragingly, and she released a tense breath. She dialed the number.

Her life was about to change forever.

Coaching Action: Awareness of the Physical Self

When was the last time you looked at yourself? When was the last time you noticed yourself? This morning? Yesterday? Hardly ever?

A good starting point when learning to master negative self-talk is to begin connecting with your body. To begin the process of building mental strength, you need to be aware of your physical self.

A great exercise for this is practicing mindfulness through mindful breathing.

Mindfulness is all about being present and being aware of how your mind and body feels. It is about acknowledging your thoughts and feelings without any judgment (Laderer, 2020).

Mindful breathing is a technique that helps us anchor ourselves in the present without our minds running off and worrying about the past or future. Being anchored in the present allows us to take a clear look at our emotions and our physical self without being bombarded by our personal judgements and biases.

Here is how to do it!

Mindful breathing doesn't have to take up much of your time. All you need is 15 minutes every day ("Mindful Breathing," 2021):

1. Find a relaxing position. This could be a comfy chair or on the floor with a cushion. When finding your position, make sure that your back is kept straight and that your hands are resting comfortably.

2. Let yourself relax and become aware of the sensations you're experiencing. Feel the floor, your chair pressing into you, and feel the air on your skin. The most important thing here is to relax any tensions.

3. Tune in to the rhythm of your breathing. Feel the air enter and exit your lungs and mouth. Feel your chest expand and contract. You don't need to do anything to control your breathing. Breath as you naturally would. While breathing, try to feel your breath in your body. See if you can feel the sensations of breathing. It might take a few tries for you to be able to do this, so don't get discouraged if it doesn't work on your first try.

4. Now, if you're a beginner to mindful breathing, it is likely that your mind will start to wander. There is nothing wrong with this. When this happens, I want you to be conscious of the fact that your mind is wandering. Once you're conscious of it, try to bring your mind back to focusing on your breathing.

5. Focus on your breathing for a few minutes and then switch back to focusing on your body and the sensations you're feeling.

The point of this exercise is to help you become more in tune with your body and the sensations you're feeling. It is to help you recognize and be aware of your physical self.

Chapter 2:

Your Reality and Vision

*H*ave you ever gotten ready for bed after a long, exhausting day and the moment you're under the covers, your mind decides to replay a highlight reel of your most embarrassing moments?

No? Just me?

Remembering the bad moments of your life—the most embarrassing moments that you've experienced—has the potential to ruin your entire day. It has the power to keep you up at night, cringing at your past self.

The experience is not pleasant.

Why does that happen? Why do we have a tendency to dwell on the past, even though we've learned from it?

This chapter aims to answer these questions, attempts to understand the human obsession with the past, and learn how this affects your present.

In this chapter, I want to highlight the importance of living in the now and not allowing yourself to be distracted by the past or the future. The key takeaway here is that you should focus on your present. Enjoy yourself in the here and now.

So often, our lives are ruled by past or future worries, and ultimately, we worry about things beyond our control.

This chapter urges you to accept your reality and plan your vision for the future. It focuses on living in the moment and not letting your past worries control your future.

Dealing With the Past

Every single one of us has experienced some form of trauma, emotional pain, or heartbreak. After all, emotional turmoil is part of the human experience. These moments of difficulty are often opportunities for us to learn and grow.

The healthy thing to do is to learn from your experiences and move on. However, what if you can't move on? What if you can't let go of the past? What is it about those memories and experiences that we can't let go of?

I've asked myself these questions more times than I can count. I've relived memories and emotions that I'd rather forget. One thing I've learned is that letting go isn't always easy. Working through our past experiences truly isn't easy.

I suppose that's why therapy exists.

For those of us who can't afford the expertise of an expensive therapist, dealing with our past is completely up to us.

In my experience, one of the best ways to move forward is to go back. Now, this might sound counterproductive, but stay with me. Often, the reason that we can't let go of the past is because we haven't made peace with it. We never got closure.

I understand why this might happen. Dealing with painful experiences is hard. It is so easy and tempting to shove our heads in the sand and wait for it to blow over. However, easy isn't always good.

Running away from our past doesn't erase it from existence. Denying the past is denying yourself the opportunity to learn from it and grow.

Here are a few reasons why going back to the past can help you move toward your future:

Take Back the Power

One of the reasons that we avoid revisiting painful memories and experiences is because we're afraid of reliving it. We don't want the bad situation to happen again (Gragg, 2020). Thinking about those experiences can fill us with too much anxiety and fear, so the easy thing to do is just avoid it.

It is easy to hide from these experiences and just hope that they go away and resolve themselves. However, in my experience, they rarely do.

What happens then is that we live our lives in fear. We might avoid certain situations or things that remind us of that traumatic time just to avoid dealing with it. This fear and anxiety becomes an unconscious part of who we are.

By facing your past, you are taking back the power to decide your future. You are no longer giving in to fear.

Owning Who You Are

Have you ever heard the saying "The past is prologue"?

Those words were penned by none other than William Shakespeare, and even though they were written centuries ago, I find that they're still relevant today.

Our pasts do not define us, but they do shape the people we become.

We are a product of all the things that have ever happened to us—that includes the good, the bad, and the ugly (Gragg, 2020). By denying your past, you are denying parts of yourself. You are living life without being fully yourself (Gragg, 2020).

Free Yourself

Carrying your past around with you, whether conscious or unconscious, becomes a weight that drags you down. It has the potential to hold you back from future opportunities and doesn't allow you to grow emotionally or mentally.

Clinging to your past can make you feel stuck, and in many ways, you are stuck.

By dealing with your past, you are able to let go of that baggage and move forward (Gragg, 2020).

Working through your past also gives you the confidence to live your life to the best of your ability.

Allowing Yourself to Heal

Holding on to the past means holding on to pain. If you are unable to deal with your past trauma and pain, they will still have an effect on you in the present (Gragg, 2020). You might employ different methods in order to avoid it.

Some of these methods can be quite harmful like substance abuse. However, as we've discussed, avoiding the problem doesn't solve it: It only makes things worse. The effect that pain has on you will increase the more you run from it. Those memories and experiences will grow and grow until it overwhelms you.

Avoiding the problem not only makes it worse but prevents you from healing. You can't heal from an experience unless you're willing to acknowledge it.

The Art of Letting Go

Now that you've faced and dealt with your past experiences, it is time to let it go and move forward. Dwelling on past events does not serve you or your future goals. In fact, it is more likely to hinder your progress and growth.

One of the major reasons that it is good to let go of the past is so that you can heal from past trauma. However, as I've mentioned, moving forward and letting go is not always easy. Here are a few tips to help you let go.

Allow Yourself to Feel the Negative Emotions

This might sound counterproductive, but in order to work through past trauma, you need to acknowledge the emotions and feelings attached to that trauma. I know that it is easier to avoid negative emotions, and allowing yourself to feel them is uncomfortable.

However, you won't be able to move forward unless you allow yourself to experience the negative emotions. Fighting them can leave you stuck in the past (Lindberg, 2018).

Handle Yourself With Care

When experiencing trauma or painful situations, you might feel the need to criticize yourself and the role you've played in that situation. However, while being self-reflective has its time and place, it is not here and not now.

When you begin your self-healing journey, you need to be kind with yourself and show yourself compassion and love (Lindberg, 2018). Treat yourself like you would a friend or loved one.

Forgive yourself for the things you couldn't control.

Distance Yourself

One of the best ways to gain a fresh perspective and move forward is to give yourself space. Allow yourself room to breathe and feel.

This could be physical space or psychological space (Lindberg, 2018). Physical space could be physically distancing yourself from the people or situation that is causing you distress by either moving or blocking their access to you.

Psychological distance could also be blocking off people's access to you by blocking them off social media or changing your phone number. This could also refer to giving yourself the mental space to experience your emotions and thoughts without any internal biases or judgment.

Practice Self-Care

Practicing self-care has become all the rage and with good reason. In our current social climate, it is easy to become absorbed in "hustle culture." Hustle culture is the need to constantly work hard. It feeds off this fast-paced environment, long working hours, and restlessness.

You're not progressing if you're not working.

I get it: We have become obsessed with proving ourselves and praising hard work. There is nothing wrong with hard work, but you cannot give your best if you are not taking care of yourself.

Using work as a means of hiding from your past experiences is not a healthy way of dealing with it. You might be telling yourself that you've moved on and are working toward something better, but the truth is that you are hiding behind work so that you don't have to deal with your past trauma.

This could lead to emotional and physical burnout; trust me, the end result isn't pretty.

Before we're able to be our best, we need to take care of ourselves. Practicing self-care looks different for everyone. For you, self-care might be setting boundaries, learning to say no, or having a bubble bath.

The point is to do what makes you feel good and what gives you the space to relax and feel safe.

Allow Yourself to Talk About It

When going through painful situations or experiencing painful emotions, it is important that you allow yourself to talk about it (Lindberg, 2018). This can be with friends or family members that you trust or through a healthcare professional.

Giving yourself the space to open up and talk about your experiences and feelings helps you work through them and make sense of what has happened. It also helps you relieve yourself of the burden of holding all those emotions in.

I know that opening up to people can be difficult. More often than not, we don't want to burden others with our problems, or we're too ashamed or embarrassed to talk about what we've been through. However, talking things through is a great way of letting your emotions out.

Talking can be as cathartic as crying. It is a physical, tangible way to release your emotions in a healthy way.

If you don't have anyone in your life that you feel comfortable enough speaking to, I'd suggest writing it all down. Begin journaling—it has a similar effect as talking without needing another person.

If you are able to, I would also recommend that you seek help from a professional. This could be a therapist or psychologist. Therapists are equipped with the tools to help you heal, and it's always great to know that you have someone in your corner.

Their professional expertise can also help guide you through the process of healing and make sense of your trauma and experiences.

Practice Mindfulness

As discussed in the first chapter, there are many benefits to practicing mindfulness. Mindfulness gives you the space to focus on yourself and your surroundings. It allows you to get in touch with your physical and mental self.

It allows you to get to know yourself.

Focusing on the present moment removes the power from past and future events. When practicing being present, the hurt we've experienced has less of an impact on our present. Practicing mindfulness also gives us the freedom to choose how we want to respond to past events (Lindberg, 2018).

Accept Reality; Plan Your Vision

One of the ways that you can move forward in life and make practical, actionable changes to improve your life is to accept your reality. Now, this might seem like a relatively easy thing to do, but often, our perception of our reality and what it truly is don't align.

We might have a completely different perception of our lives than what is really happening. We might think we're doing better than we are or worse than we are. This might be because we're in denial about our reality, we are experiencing feelings of regret or disappointment, or we could be waiting for something better (Zeman, 2019).

Failing to accurately perceive our reality is why some of us still have jeans that haven't fit in years or are stuck in a job we secretly hate.

Acknowledging your reality is the first step to improving it (Zeman, 2019).

Why Accepting Your Reality Is Important

The biggest reason why accepting your reality is important is because in order to improve your life and well-being, you need to acknowledge your current situation. Rejecting the reality of your situation doesn't change it (Zeman, 2019).

In fact, rejecting your reality and living in denial is a surefire way to ensure that you never move forward.

You're stuck having to experience the same negative emotions you've been trying to get rid of.

Have you ever heard of radical acceptance?

Radical acceptance works on the premise that you should accept things the way they are (Zeman, 2019). Practicing radical acceptance helps you accept the reality of your situation; in doing so, it also helps you figure out how to respond.

Instead of lamenting the world and screaming, "Why me?" accept that this is the way things are. The first step here is accepting that not everything is in your control.

Racial acceptance was something that I took a while to wrap my head around. I am a control freak by nature, and having to accept that there were things beyond my control wasn't easy. However, allowing myself to recognize that there are tangible things that I could control helped.

Realizing that I couldn't control everything that happened to me but that I could control my reaction to those things filled me with a sense of peace. If the only thing I could control was myself, I didn't have to worry about the actions of others. It was quite relieving if I'm being honest.

It took the pressure off and allowed me to better accept certain situations and the actions of other people.

Realizing that I was finally in control of my life and my future was freeing made me feel like I wasn't responsible for anyone else.

The same thing applies to you. You are only responsible for yourself. You control your life and the direction it takes. Accepting that there are things you cannot control and taking responsibility for the things you can control is the first step toward improving your life.

Ultimately, my advice is to accept your reality. Face it head-on and stare all those flaws and weaknesses down. Accept them in all their horrible glory and be grateful that you are able to see them. Your current reality is your starting point. It is your jumping board propelling you forward.

After all, you can't move forward without knowing where you begin.

Your Vision

Now that you've accepted your reality and acknowledged it for what it is, it's time to think about what you truly want it to be. What do you want your life to look like overall? What do you really want your future to look like?

What is your vision for your life?

Your vision can include tangible goals such as career and lifestyle aspirations, and it can include intangible goals such as improving your mental and physical well-being. Your vision for your future might be to improve your mental health and live a happier, more fulfilling life.

Whatever your vision, it is time to begin actively reaching for it. It is easy to simply dream about the life you want; what's hard is working toward that life. Often, this means stepping out of our comfort zone and putting ourselves in uncomfortable situations.

If your goal is to improve your physical health, that might require you to get up earlier in order to go to the gym. This alone will upset your routine. However, what I want you to realize is that large-scale, long-term change isn't easy—it's uncomfortable and scary.

Here are a few tips to help you face these changes head-on and achieve your vision:

Figure Out What's Not Working

The first step when you begin actively working toward changing your life for the better is looking at your current situation and figuring out what isn't working. Identify the aspects of your life that might be holding you back. These could be habits that you've picked up or larger aspects of your lifestyle.

The point here is to identify the aspects of your life that are no longer serving you. Ask yourself what you need to change in order for you to achieve your vision.

You could physically note the things you need to change via journaling or mind mapping. This gives you a great visual of the things in your life that are not working.

A good way to assess whether something is serving you or not is looking at whether they are in line with your core values and ideals.

Make a Mind Map

Mind maps are a great way to organize your thoughts and figure out what you value. Mind mapping your thoughts and values gives you a visual perspective of what you consider important. You could also use this method to figure out what you want out of life.

When using a mind map, you can sketch out your big-picture goals. These are generally large-scale, long-term goals. It is a good place to start when you begin setting goals.

Set Realistic Goals

Once you've figured out your vision and decided on what you want out of life, it is finally time to set your goals. Though it's natural to be excited to begin a new chapter in your life, this excitement can cause you to set unrealistic goals.

You might set out to have an entire career change within the next few months, or aim to own a beach house within the next year. While there is nothing inherently wrong with these goals, depending on your personal capabilities, they might be unrealistic.

If you're living paycheck to paycheck, affording a beach house within a year is not a realistic goal. If you've worked the same job for years, switching careers won't be a walk in the park.

Setting unrealistic goals is setting yourself up for failure.

I would advise that, when setting goals, you take your capabilities into account. What can you realistically achieve within a year?

If you want that beach house, how much will you need to save toward a mortgage? How long will it take you to reach that amount?

When setting goals, it is best to start small and work your way up to bigger goals. In fact, I would advise that you break up that large goal into smaller goals, so they can act as milestones.

Not only will this keep you motivated to work toward these goals but it will act as a road map and keep you focused.

Living in the Moment: Mindfulness

We've spoken about mindfulness in the previous chapter, and I've given you a coaching action on mindful breathing. In this section, I'd like to expand on the concept of mindfulness and discuss the importance of truly living in the moment.

Living in the moment sounds wonderful. It gives me the feeling of being carefree and living without stress and anxiety. While being mindful and living in the moment does aid with reducing unnecessary stress and anxiety, I want you to remember that we're all human.

Anxiety and stress are as much a part of being human as breathing. I don't want you to have unrealistic expectations of living mindfully. Living in the moment and practicing mindfulness isn't automatically going to solve your life problems. It is not a magic cure-all.

What it is will be a tool to help you manage your overall stress and anxiety and improve your well-being. Like all tools, its effectiveness depends on how you use it.

If you're practicing mindfulness, it can have amazing benefits. Living in the moment has been shown to reduce stress and anxiety which can help you avoid conditions such as high blood pressure, obesity, and heart disease (Francis, 2013).

It also has the potential to improve your relationships. Being both physically and mentally present can help you form meaningful connections with the people in your life. It can also help you better understand the people around you and the effect they have on you.

Being mentally present also increases your enjoyment of another's company.

The greatest benefit to practicing mindfulness is improved mental well-being. Mindful meditation is a great way of improving your mental health and reducing symptoms of depression and anxiety.

But how does one practice mindfulness?

There are numerous methods to practicing mindfulness. One that we've already covered is mindful breathing. Additional methods include mindful walking, mindful meditation, and mindful activities.

In the coaching action of this chapter, I will discuss mindful meditation and give you a step-by-step guide on how to practice it.

The Actress and I

Amelia held the phone up to her ear. Her eyes nervously glancing around the room. I watched her carefully; I know exactly how much she's overcome to reach this moment. I know just how many difficult conversations she'd had to have with herself to get to this point, so I'm very proud of her.

She is much stronger than she thinks she is.

Up until this point, not much has gone right in her life. She's been passed up on awards and lead roles. She's been overlooked by directors in favor of more famous actresses, and when she first came to me, she assumed she'd always be stuck on the C-list. She assumed she'd always be playing the best friend or rival.

Amelia wanted to be an A-list actress but was unsure what she should do to reach that goal.

I told her what I tell all of my clients: If you want a different outcome, you're going to need to use a different strategy. Something in your life needs to change.

I heard the phone ringing, and on the other end of the line, someone picked up.

"Hello?"

Coaching Action: Awareness of Your Surroundings Excersie)

Now that we've practiced mindful breathing and getting in touch with our physical selves, I want you to expand your awareness outward. Focus on your surroundings. Focus on your inner thoughts and feelings. What are you thinking? What are you feeling?

There are two methods that I find particularly effective when expanding your awareness. The first is mindful meditation, which works well if you want to closely examine your thoughts. The second is mindful walking, which is a great method to help you become more aware of your surroundings in the long run.

The great thing about practicing mindfulness is that often, these techniques and methods can be combined. You can practice mindful breathing while practicing mindful meditation. You can also practice mindful meditation while practicing mindful walking.

Now, I want you to switch off your phone and remove yourself from distractions. Shift your focus to your surroundings and simply look around.

What are you thinking? What are you feeling?

Spend around two minutes observing the world around you. If you can, I'd recommend that you go on a walk and keep observing your surroundings.

The aim of this exercise is to help you become aware of your thoughts and surroundings.

Chapter 3:

Self-Talk

We all have an inner voice—the little voice at the back of your head that delivers a running commentary on your life, your experiences, and your actions. While you might not have been actively practicing self-talk, your inner voice has always been with you.

Your inner voice influences how you see yourself and the world around you.

This chapter aims to understand what self-talk is and why we have it.

What is the purpose of self-talk? How does it help us navigate life? These are the questions I aim to answer in this chapter.

I also look at the different kinds of self-talk and the impact they have on our mental and emotional well-being.

Often, I have found that our inner voices have more of an effect on our lives and our sense of self than we think. Identifying your inner-voice and realizing what kind of self-talk you are engaging in is a good starting point for improving your self-confidence.

The title of this book is *Shut Up!*, and as mentioned in the introduction, it is aimed at helping you identify and control your inner voice. The goal is to have your inner voice shut up if it is being negative and bringing you down.

In this chapter, I define self-talk and go on to discuss positive and negative self-talk. I also address the issue of imposter syndrome and submodalities.

I then continue with the story of Amelia the actress.

This chapter ends with a coaching action that has you focusing on the person who means the most to you.

What Is Self-Talk?

In simple terms, self-talk is your inner monologue—it is your inner voice. Oftentimes, your inner voice reflects your internal biases and judgments. Self-talk is something that people do naturally throughout the day.

This could be planning our day mentally, making mental shopping lists, or simply reminding yourself of things that need your attention (Morris, 2016). Self-talk could also be a running commentary of your day, what you're thinking, or what you're feeling.

One thing I want to make clear is that self-talk does not always reflect your true feelings or opinions. They are more likely to express learned biases that might have been passed down from your parents or be reflective of things that you are constantly hearing.

As much as your inner self-talk can reflect how you see your surroundings, it is also a product of your surroundings and environment (Morris, 2016).

Generally, there are three different kinds of self-talk. There is positive self-talk, negative self-talk, and neutral self-talk.

In this chapter, I will be focusing on positive and negative self-talk.

Neutral self-talk is what I like to think of as general observations that you make throughout the day. Things like realizing you're cold or that there's a new scent in the air. Basically, these are thoughts that have neither a positive nor negative connotation.

Positive and Negative Self-Talk

Everyone experiences positive and negative self-talk. It is completely natural to have positive and negative thoughts; after all, we're only human.

The issue arises when one overpowers the other. Too much positive self-talk can lead to toxic positivity, and too much negative self-talk can lead to feelings of stress, depression, and anxiety.

Both are equally harmful to your mental and emotional well-being.

There is a key difference between positive and negative self-talk. Positive self-talk allows you to look at the bright side and encourages you (7 Summit Pathways, 2019). It tells you things like, "You've done well today," or "You might not have achieved all your goals, but you'll do better tomorrow."

On the other hand, negative self-talk makes you feel bad about yourself. Negative self-talk says things like, "You didn't complete your to-do list; you're so lazy," or, "You failed that test; you're not smart enough to be doing this." With negative self-talk, the things we tell ourselves often stem from the negative things others have said to us. These negative things replay in our minds on a constant loop until we begin hearing that message from ourselves (7 Summit Pathways, 2019). It is no longer others bringing us down: We begin bringing ourselves down.

Positive Self-Talk

As mentioned, positive self-talk is an inner voice that makes us feel good about ourselves and our environment. Positive self-talk is focused on treating yourself with kindness and compassion (Estrada, 2020).

Thinking positively and focusing on the positive aspects of our lives can help us mitigate the effects of stress and anxiety and fend off feelings of depression. It also greatly improves your quality of life (Holland, 2018).

A few of the tangible benefits positive self-talk can generate include:

- increased satisfaction with your life
- better physical and mental well-being
- decreased feelings of stress and anxiety
- increased vitality

It is not clear why having positive self-talk and being optimistic produces these effects, but it could be a testament to mind over matter.

People who have positive-self talk are also better at solving problems and are more efficient at working through times of hardships and difficulty (Holland, 2018).

How to Practice Positive Self-Talk

If you're not used to practicing positive-self talk, it can be quite difficult to begin. Practicing positive self-talk requires shifting your mindset and changing the way you think about yourself, your environment, and others.

It is about recognizing your failures as learning opportunities and seeing your flaws as opportunities for growth.

Here are a few tips on how to begin practicing positive self-talk:

1. **Start small:** By starting small, you won't get overwhelmed by trying to change many things at once. Instead of jumping into the deep end, dip your toes into the shallow end by practicing positive self-talk in one area of your life. This could be practicing self-talk with regard to your work or perhaps your personal life. Perhaps you'd like to improve your self-love or confidence.

   I would advise that you start with the area of yourself you tend to judge harshly. If you struggle with body positivity or confidence, you could begin working on those areas.

   The key with practicing positive self-talk is to make sure it is realistic and authentic (Estrada, 2020). Make it believable.

For example, if you want to work on self-love, you could begin with thoughts like "I am a person; I deserve respect." This is a very basic statement that can make a world of difference to your self-confidence.

Once you're comfortable with that statement, you can move on to larger statements like, "I am beautiful inside and out."

2. **Avoid comparing yourself to others:** It is easy to put yourself down when you start comparing yourself to others (Battles, 2016). When comparing yourself to others, it is easy to find yourself lacking and thinking things like, "I'll never be as successful as that person," or "I'm not as pretty as that person."

Rather than looking at others and focusing on what you think you're lacking, try to be grateful for what you have (Battles, 2016). Shift your focus from others and back to yourself. You might not have a luxury beachfront apartment, but you have a warm house to come home to. You might not have a supermodel figure, but your body is strong and healthy.

3. **Make changes to your behavior:** Practicing positive self-talk and positive thinking is a great first step; however, it is not enough on its own. Positive self-talk needs to be backed up with new behaviors that reinforces the changes you want to make to your life

Basically, it is not enough to talk the talk: You've got to walk the walk.

For example, if you're practicing positive self-talk with regard to body positivity, in addition to positive affirmations, what actions can you take to show your body love (Estrada, 2020)? You could take action by doing physical exercises, eating healthy, or implementing a skincare routine.

4. **Seek professional help:** If you are struggling with negative self-talk and are hitting mental blocks when you try implementing positive self-talk, you might want to consider seeking professional help (Estrada, 2020).

The prevalence of negative self-talk could be an indication of deeper issues such as depression. Having the aid of a professional could help you dig deeper into the causes of your negative self-talk and implement strategies to practice positive self-talk.

Practicing positive self-talk can often feel uncomfortable, especially if you're not used to treating yourself gently and with kindness. It will not be easy, and the benefits of positive self-talk will not happen overnight. I would advise you to be patient with yourself and move at a pace that works for you.

Negative Self-Talk

Negative self-talk can take many forms, and more often than not, it is not as mean as it sounds. Negative self-talk can sound like the musings of your inner critic (Scott, 2018). It could say things like, "You're not good at that; you should stop doing it," and at first glance, that doesn't sound so bad. Why should you try something if you're not good at it? However, the problem with this kind of thinking is that it limits what you're able to do. It also holds you back from exploring new, exciting things.

Negative self-talk is any internal dialogue that limits your ability to believe in yourself and reach your potential (Scott, 2018). Negative self-talk diminishes your ability to make positive changes in your life and lowers your confidence.

Frequently engaging in negative self-talk can have harmful effects on your mental health. It can increase feelings of stress, anxiety, and could lead to depression.

Negative self-talk can also alter your perception of reality. You might perceive your environment and the people around you as being more hostile and colder than they actually are due to your own preconceived notions.

Here are a few consequences of negative self-talk:

- Limited thinking: If you don't believe that you can do something, chances are you won't be able to do it. Constantly telling yourself that you're unable to achieve something m: you believe that it is true.

- Feelings of anxiety and depression: Being constantly bombarded with negative thoughts and comments can lead to increased feelings of anxiety and depression. After all, you can't be optimistic and positive when you're constantly surrounded by negativity.

- Damage to relationships: Experiencing constant self-criticism can make you come across as needy and insecure in your relationships. You could also become increasingly sensitive to any form of criticism from others which could make you lash out.

Characteristics of Negative Self-Talk

In order to combat negative self-talk, you first need to be able to identify it. By knowing what to look out for, you'll be able to address these thoughts and combat them by implementing positive self-talk.

A few key characteristics of negative self-talk include:

1. **Assuming you know what others are thinking and feeling:** A characteristic of negative self-talk is assuming that you understand the thoughts and feelings of others. It is imagining that people are thinking or feeling negatively about you without any sound evidence. Often, this is a projection of your own negative feelings and insecurities.

2. **Overgeneralization:** Overgeneralization occurs when you believe that a negative event is bound to happen again (Scott, 2018). This can cause you to make predictions about the future that are based on isolated incidents. Imagine that you're passed over for a job you really wanted. You could say things like, "I'm never going to find a job," or, "I'm never going to be successful." These are large statements about your future based on a single negative interaction.

   The harm here is that this kind of thinking influences your perception of your future and could prevent you from achieving your goals—kind of like a prophecy for self-actualization.

3. **Black-and-white thinking:** Black-and-white thinking is the habit of evaluating things based on preconceived categories. These categories are often extremes of good and bad. Black and white thinking commonly occurs when we think about ourselves, our characteristics, or qualities.

   For example, you could say things like, "I am *so* awkward" after experiencing a negative interaction.

   The issue here is that black-and-white thinking sets you up for chronic disappointment. You'll never be able to live up to the ideals you've set up, and you'll beat yourself up for not being able to meet them (Scott, 2018).

4. **Magnification:** Magnification is one of the most common characteristics of negative self-talk. Magnification is the habit of taking your flaws, shortcomings, and mistakes and inflating them (Scott, 2018). This makes them seem larger and more prominent than they actually are. Magnification turns an ant hill into a mountain.

   For example, you could forget someone's name and think, *"Oh man, I'm such an idiot! They must hate me now.*

   The issue with magnification is that it clouds our perception of ourselves and our environment. Our every mistake is magnified until it becomes the only thing we are able to focus on.

When examining your thoughts and internal monologue, keep an eye out for this kind of thinking. It is also a good idea to monitor the frequency of these kinds of thoughts. I would advise that if you find yourself experiencing frequent negative self-talk, combat it with positive self-talk.

For example, if you're thinking, *I'm an idiot*, combat that thought with something like, *I am trying my best, and I am still learning. I will improve over time.*

Imposter Syndrome

Imposter syndrome is closely linked to negative self-talk and can be seen as one of the consequences of negative self-talk or an aspect of negative self-talk.

Imposter syndrome can be described as an internal belief or experience that you are not as competent as others think you are (Cuncic, 2020). It can also be thought of as believing that you are undeserving of the position you hold. Imposter syndrome is closely linked to perfectionism and feeling as though you'll never measure up to a certain standard.

Basically, imposter syndrome is feeling like a phony. It is as though, at any moment, the people around you are going to realize that you're a fraud, or you're not as smart or as capable as they thought you were.

Imposter syndrome can affect anyone, no matter their skill level, experience, or achievements.

For some, experiencing imposter syndrome can be a huge motivator to work harder and improve themselves. However, this comes at the cost of constant feelings of anxiety. This might push you to work harder so that "no one finds out you're a fraud," but, no matter how much you work, it'll never be enough.

Doing well or achieving something means nothing in the face of imposter syndrome. You might even rationalize it by saying, "I got lucky," or, "The only reason I did well was because the task was made easier." Imposter syndrome completely disregards the work you've put into something, your own skills and abilities, and your achievements.

Everything you achieve is based purely on luck or the goodwill of others. Imposter syndrome will never give you any credit.

Key characteristics of imposter syndrome include:

- self-doubt
- increased feelings of insecurity
- the fear that you will never live up to expectations

- the inability to realistically assess your abilities and skills

- attributing your success to other external factors

Imposter syndrome is a conflict between how you perceive yourself and how others perceive you. Others might value your contribution and expertise, but your own internal perceptions prevent you from seeing that.

Over time, experiencing imposter syndrome can lead to increased feelings of anxiety, guilt, and depression (Saripalli, 2021). It could also lead to increased feelings of insecurity and be damaging to your self-confidence.

There are five types of imposter syndrome that you could experience:

The Expert

This kind of imposter syndrome is characterized by the belief that your competence is based on what you know and how much you know. It is also the belief that your competence is based on what you're able to do and how much you're able to do (Wilding, 2017).

This leads to living with the fear that you'll never know enough, and you'll never be doing enough. It is the fear that you'll be exposed for being stupid and incompetent.

This kind of imposter syndrome is commonly experienced by professionals and in the workplace. You might believe that you got the job you have by accident, or you're not really qualified for that position.

This kind of thinking could also cause you to miss out on opportunities because you believe that you don't meet the necessary requirements.

People who experience this kind of imposter syndrome might be driven to constantly improve themselves and increase their skill set so that they won't be found to be a "fraud" (Wilding, 2017).

While improving yourself and increasing your skill set is never a bad thing, pushing yourself too hard could lead to mental and physical burnout.

The Superhero

The superhero kind of imposter syndrome is characterized by the belief that you are a fraud among experts. This often stems from deep feelings of insecurity and a lack of self-confidence.

People with the superhero imposter syndrome might view their colleagues or the people around them as being experts in their field. This perception is also easily inflated by viewing these people as being superheroes in their field.

In contrast, you view yourself as being a sidekick masquerading as a superhero.

This could lead to you working harder than the people around you. It could also lead to you becoming a workaholic that thrives on the external validation you get from working yourself to the bone.

You might jump at the chance to work overtime or overload yourself with projects in order to prove yourself to others.

If this sounds like you, I would advise that you shift your focus from the external to the internal. What I mean by this is that you should try to veer away from external validation and try to nurture your inner confidence.

The Perfectionist

The perfectionist is a close partner of imposter syndrome. They go hand in hand. Perfectionism, by definition, is holding yourself to an unrealistic standard. You might set high goals for yourself and then experience heavy feelings of self-doubt and self-loathing when you fail to meet these goals.

Simply put, you hold yourself to a perceived standard of perfection. Often, this standard is unreachable.

The perfectionist sets impossible goals and essentially sets themselves up for failure. Any successes that you achieve are rarely satisfying, and you constantly believe that you could've done better (Wilding, 2017).

The perfectionist leaves no room for error, so mistakes are inconceivable. This kind of thinking could lead to you becoming a control freak and trying to micromanage everything and everyone in your life in order to achieve *perfection*.

What I want you to realize is that perfection is an illusion. We can only do our best, learn from our mistakes, and ultimately, try to improve. Fighting for perfection is playing a losing game because nothing you do will never live up to your perceived standard.

The Soloist

The soloist kind of imposter syndrome is defined by their belief that if they ask for help or assistance, that this will reveal them to be a "fraud." While independence is an important part of our development, asking for help is definitely not a sign of weakness.

People who experience this form of imposter syndrome often refuse any form of help or assistance and insist on doing things on their own, even if they struggle to do so.

If you are battling with this kind of imposter syndrome, it is important for you to realize that there is truly no shame in asking for help. If you don't know how to do something or need help, ask for it.

By denying help, you are denying yourself the opportunity to learn and improve yourself.

The Natural Genius

The natural genius form of imposter syndrome causes people to believe that they need to be naturally capable or good at things. This causes them to judge their abilities and competence based on the ease and speed that they're able to tackle tasks with instead of their own efforts (Wilding, 2017).

Much like the perfectionist, the natural genius sets the performance bar pretty high. They judge their competency based on how quickly they're able to complete tasks. If they're unable to complete tasks the first time around, it can be quite upsetting.

The point here is to get things right the first time.

In order to combat this kind of thinking, I would advise that you begin seeing yourself as a work in progress. Life is a continuous learning journey, and we are always growing and improving. There is nothing wrong with struggling; there is no shame in struggling.

Submodalities

Have you ever wondered why you believe what you believe and why you may perceive the world differently than others? Well, the answer, while not simple, stems from modalities and submodalities.

Submodalities are a tricky concept to wrap your head around. When I first learned about submodalities, it took me a while to understand exactly what the point was. The language often got so technical, I got headaches just looking at the words.

To save you the headache I endured, I've dumbed down the concept.

In simple terms, submodalities, in the world of neuro-linguistic programming, refers to the distinctions made between different modalities. Modalities refer to visual, auditory, olfactory, gustatory, and kinesthetic systems that give meaning to the human experience ("Submodalities," 2012).

An example of the visual modality would be your eyes, your nervous system, your ocular nerves, and the parts of your brain that process visual stimuli.

Your olfactory modality concerns your sense of smell, and your auditory modality refers to your hearing.

In simple terms, modalities refer to the systems that allow you to perceive the world around you. The submodalities are how we understand and structure those perceptions and experiences.

Humans are able to create meaning by implementing different submodalities in order to code our experiences. For example, this could be our likes, dislikes, and our personal preferences.

Due to the impact submodalities have in shaping our perception of the world, shifting our submodalities is an effective method of changing the meaning of our experiences ("Submodalities," 2012).

Submodalities have a huge effect on both negative and positive self-talk. After all, much of how we perceive other people has to do with their tone of voice, their appearance, and our own personal biases.

With regard to negative self-talk, using an auditory swish pattern can help people combat that nagging negative internal voice. The idea is to target people's internal biases about the kind of voice that they find motivating and using that to combat negative self-talk (Livingston, 2019).

In simple terms, auditory swish patterns aim to change the tone of your internal voice so that it sounds more positive and motivating, even if the words it is saying aren't that positive.

For example, your negative self-talk might say something like, "How did that happen?" in a tone that you perceive as accusing and angry. By shifting the tone to something calm and understanding, it changes the meaning and impression that those words give you.

The Actress and I

Amelia whispers a hello back before clearing her throat and answering with more confidence.

I can tell that she's still nervous and unsure of herself. With her free hand, she fiddles with the phone cord. Her bright eyes darted around the room, never quite settling. She has suffered for a long time—weighed down by feelings of self-doubt and insecurity.

It has taken her a long time to reach this point and I know that she has the strength to follow through with her plan.

During one of our sessions, I implored her to think about why she thought she was struggling through auditions. It took a while, but finally, she confided in me that she thought her friend was a better actress.

"She knows all her lines and always puts on a believable performance," Amelia told me, hanging her head.

"I feel like I'm always competing against someone else," she said.

"And is that competition close to you?" I asked.

She considered my words carefully; a look of recognition came across her face.

And there it was—the heart of her problem.

Amelia's negative internal dialogue was sabotaging her at every turn. It made her nervous and caused her to lose focus.

I hoped that all that would change with this phone call.

Coaching Action: Awareness of Your Positive Thoughts About Another Person

Who is your role model? Who is the person you most admire? What about them warrants your admiration?

One of the people that I admire is Phil Jackson, a legendary NBA coach who coached one of the greatest basketball players, Michael Jordan. Michael Jordan was one of the most gifted players the NBA had ever seen, and yet, he had never won a championship until Phil Jackson took over the coaching reins.

Jackson entered with a new perspective and encouraged Jordan to place more trust in his teammates and be less stingy with the ball. His idea was that teams won championships, not players.

How right he was.

Together, Jackson and the team went on to win six NBA championships!

Thinking about Phil Jackson always makes me feel positive and hopeful. If I close my eyes, I can hear the words *winner*, *influence*, and *calm*.

Keeping this in mind, here is what I want you to do.

Turn off your phone and remove yourself from all distractions.

I want you to think about the person you admire the most. Think about why you admire them and what it is about them that you admire.

What words and images come to mind?

The idea behind this exercise is to help you focus on positive thoughts. I want you to be aware of how positive thoughts make you feel.

Chapter 4:

Expectations

If you type the word "expectation" into Google, the first definition that comes up says it's a "strong belief that something will happen or be the case" ("Expectation," 2021). While that is the gist of it, expectations and having expectations are so much more than that.

We wake up every day with a set of expectations all prepared and ready to go. We expect the sun to rise. If we are employed, we expect to get to work. We expect to eat breakfast and see friends, and a dozen other things. Mostly, we have an unconscious expectation that our day will go according to plan.

If you're anything like me, planning is everything. I plan out my days, weeks, months, and sometimes my year way too far in advance, and I've always done this with the expectation that things will go my way.

I plan with the expectation that my future self will stick to those plans and that I'll achieve my goals.

However, just because we expect something to happen doesn't necessarily mean it will. If there's anything that I've learned in life it's that nothing is set in stone.

Even with that in mind, we continue to live our lives with expectations. We have a tendency to pile our hopes and aspirations on expectations. This could be expectations on how the people around us act, our expectations of the future, or the expectations we have for our relationships.

What feels strange to me is that we know expectation does not equal certainty, yet we hold such hope that it does. There is nothing wrong with having expectations; there is nothing wrong with planning for the future either. It is human nature to want to plan and ensure that we reach our goals and dreams.

The issue arises when our expectations don't align with reality. It becomes an issue when we expect things to happen without having any evidence to suggest that it will.

For example, let's say you have an important test coming up. You fully expect to pass that test. You might not be worried about how well you do but you expect to pass. However, instead of studying for the test, you decide to wing it. In the end, you end up failing the test, and you're upset.

In this instance, you held an expectation but nothing in your behavior or environment reinforced that expectation. You didn't study or prepare to take that test—your expectations and your reality were misaligned.

This chapter discusses unrealistic expectations and the misalignment of expectations and reality. It also looks at the expectations you have of others and their expectations of you.

This chapter is closely linked with the previous chapter. Often, our negative self-talk stems from having unrealistic expectations or having our expectations and perceptions misalign with reality.

In this chapter, I'll also discuss the importance of setting realistic expectations and how to set realistic expectations.

As always, this chapter ends off with a snippet of our story with the actress and a coaching action.

Misalignments of Expectations

When our expectations and reality misalign, it can be quite frustrating. After all, we place our hopes and aspirations on expectations, and when they fall through, it can be devastating.

While we might recognize the gap between our reality and our expectations, more often than not, we miss it completely and internalize the failure. We didn't meet the deadline because we're lazy, or we missed an appointment because we're disorganized. We make the failure our fault.

This kind of thinking is closely linked to negative self-talk.

In addition to the expectations we have of our reality, we also hold expectations of the people around us and our relationships. Chances are that the people around us have expectations of us as well.

Our expectations are also the basis on which we assess whether we're satisfied or not. This applies to our jobs, relationships, and the environment we find ourselves in. It affects every aspect of our lives.

What happens when our expectations don't line up with reality? How do we close the gap between expectation and reality, and how do we prevent it from happening again?

Expectations vs. Reality

The misalignment of expectation and reality is a common occurrence—more common than you might think.

Have you ever checked out a restaurant and looked through their online menu? The pictures of their food set up certain expectations in your mind. You expect that the food you receive looks like the picture. You also expect the food to taste exactly like, or better, than what you imagined.

If you go to the restaurant and find the food lacking, it is likely that you'll be disappointed. Your expectations weren't met, and the reality wasn't what you expected.

A major struggle that we constantly face is the mismatch between expectation and reality. When this mismatch occurs, it can be quite upsetting.

The introduction of social media hasn't made this easier. Every day, we're bombarded with the seemingly perfect lives of others and are left wondering why our realities don't match theirs.

We could've had expectations about where we'd be at certain points in our lives, and once we reach those points and compare our reality with our expectation, there are often glaring gaps. This leaves us wondering what we did wrong. Where did we go wrong?

The worst-case scenario in this instance would be that we expect our lives to be headed in one direction when the reality might be that we're heading in the complete opposite direction without realizing it.

A key cause of experiencing a misalignment between your expectations and your reality could be because you're setting unrealistic expectations for yourself and your environment.

Unrealistic Expectations

One of the reasons that your expectations aren't lining up with your reality could be because the expectations you hold are unrealistic. There are many reasons why you could have unrealistic expectations.

It could be that you're comparing your life to others, you could be seeking external validation, or it could be that you have a warped perspective of yourself and your life.

Whatever the reason, setting unrealistic expectations might cause you to be working toward something or putting extensive effort toward something without seeing any progress.

For example, you could spend tons of cash on lottery tickets expecting to win without much thought behind it, or you could be expecting to find a rom-com movie. These expectations are unrealistic and are based more in fantasy than fact. This could have negative effects on your life and your well-being such as experiencing feelings of anxiety, inadequacy, or frustration.

The point I'm trying to make is that setting unrealistic expectations can be setting yourself up for ultimate failure. If you are constantly unable to meet these unrealistic expectations, you might give up and stop trying.

However, is there a way we can avoid this? How do we let go of unrealistic expectations and align our expectations with our reality?

One of the ways to do this is by practicing mindfulness. Living in the moment! Being aware of your surroundings and the events happening to you.

Here are a few tips on how to align your expectations with your reality:

1. Building Awareness

One of the best ways to align your expectations with your reality is by taking a deep look at how your expectations measure up to your reality. Where are the gaps? How big are those gaps? What might be causing them?

When entering a new situation, ask yourself what your expectations are. Then, question whether these expectations you hold are realistic or not (Scott, 2020). Ask yourself why you hold those expectations in the first place.

If the expectations you have are of yourself, examine your capabilities. What are you realistically capable of?

For example, if you've set a deadline for yourself, ask yourself if you can realistically reach that deadline. Do you have enough time? Have you left room for error? Have you considered your capabilities?

These questions can help keep you grounded in reality and prevent you from setting unrealistic expectations.

2. Managing Your Expectations

The core of aligning your expectations with reality comes down to expanding your awareness. When entering a new situation or environment, being aware of what you're expecting is a great way to start (Scott, 2020).

In addition to being aware of what you're expecting, you should also be aware of what you should be expecting from this situation. Ask yourself what realistic expectations you should have in this situation.

For example, when you start a new job, a few realistic expectations that you should have can be getting paid regularly and being respected in the workplace. None of these expectations are unreasonable or unrealistic.

However, as I've mentioned before, just because you expect something to happen doesn't mean it will. Therefore, when you find that things aren't going the way you expected, I would advise you to try and look at the positives of what you have.

Once you've overcome your initial disappointment, you might find that you have something you didn't realize you wanted (Scott, 2020).

This practice helps you appreciate what you have instead of focusing on what you don't.

However, while it is good practice to manage your expectations, I do not want you to forget your worth. When reasonable expectations aren't met, it has nothing to do with you, but it has everything to do with the situation and the people involved.

For example, if you're doing good work at your job and aren't being fairly paid, this isn't a reflection on you.

3. Focus On Your Achievements

As I've mentioned, having unrealistic expectations can be setting yourself up for failure. Constantly failing to meet these expectations can seriously mess with your self-confidence and leave you feeling frustrated.

When that happens, I want you to focus on the things you have achieved. Revisit your accomplishments and see how far you've grown.

Keeping your accomplishments in the rearview mirror is a great way of helping you keep things in perspective. This also allows you to carve out a space to appreciate yourself and appreciate your accomplishments.

How to Set Realistic Expectations

Up until now, I haven't been inspiring confidence in setting expectations. I've spoken about all the bad things associated with having expectations and why you should avoid having unrealistic expectations.

However, as with most things, having expectations has its pros and cons—the cons stemming from unrealistic expectations and the pros from having realistic expectations.

Having goals and setting realistic expectations and intentions for yourself are essential for both professional and personal development (Yang, 2021). Setting realistic expectations and goals gives you something to work toward. In some ways, it can give you a sense of purpose and guide your day-to-day life.

But how does one set realistic expectations?

Evaluate Your Life

Take a good look at your life and ask yourself a few questions. What in your life brings you joy? What is causing you frustration and stress? What aspects of your life are working, and what aspects aren't working? What do you want more of? What do you want less of?

These questions are a great way of determining your level of satisfaction and identifying the aspects of your life that need changing. When you're evaluating your life, I'd also like you to look forward and think about the life you want to lead.

What are the key differences between what you want and what you have? Is your ideal life a realistic possibility? If so, what needs to change for you to reach those expectations?

Once you know what you want out of life and in which direction you want to go, you can start using that to begin setting your goals (Yang, 2021).

Evaluate Your Expectations

In the first tip mentioned, I asked you to envision your ideal life. With that imagination comes a certain set of expectations. Now, before you begin setting goals to reach those expectations, I want you to pause for a moment.

Are the expectations you have about your ideal future realistic? Is the future you envision attainable? How far are these expectations from reality? Are there any gaps?

Carefully evaluate your expectations and determine whether or not they're realistic (Yang, 2021). After all, there's no point in working toward an unrealistic or fantasy-filled future. You do not want to set yourself up for disappointment.

If you're still unsure about whether your expectations are realistic or not, refer to the beginning of this chapter and follow the steps mentioned.

Identify Your Values

What is it that you value the most? Your values can be tangible or intangible. It could include having your personal boundaries respected or being able to have a massage once a week. Whatever your values are, your expectations and goals should align with them.

Therefore, before you set your goals, I want you to think about what you value most and list them. Now, you can employ various methods to do this such as the mind map method mentioned earlier. No matter the method, the outcome should be the same.

By the end of this exercise, you should be left with a list of the things that you value most.

Identifying your values gives you some guidelines when setting your goals. Knowing your values is also a great way of managing your expectations.

Be Realistic

Now, this goes without saying, but ensure that your expectations and the goals you set are realistic. When setting goals, it is easy to veer off the path of realism and enter a fantasy world.

It is exciting to imagine yourself achieving fantastic feats and reaching amazing levels of success, but while it is fun to imagine, this doesn't do much, practically speaking. Imagining our goals does not help us achieve them.

I would also advise that you're honest with yourself about your capabilities and what you're realistically able to achieve.

Remember to Remain Mindful

With all this talk of setting goals and expectations, it can be easy to become lost in thoughts of the future. While thinking about the future and all the possibilities it holds can be exciting, I don't want you to forget about the present.

As I've mentioned before, practicing mindfulness is a great way to keep yourself rooted in the present and remain in touch with reality.

Remaining mindful can also help you align your expectations with your reality.

How to Deal With Other People's Expectations of You

Now, just because you've learned to manage your expectations in order to keep them rooted in reality doesn't mean the people around you have done the same. Chances are that the people around you hold as much expectations about themselves and their environment as you do.

More often than not, the people in your life have set expectations of you as well—whether you're aware of it or not. The expectations that others have of you starts as soon as you're born and perhaps even before birth.

The first expectations that others could attach to you are gendered. If you're born a boy, chances are that your parents and family members have certain expectations of you. They could expect you to fit the socially acceptable role of being a boy by playing sports, being active and athletic, and being strong and assertive.

If you're born a girl, those closest to you could expect you to fulfill the socially acceptable role of being a girl by being quiet and neat, by playing with dolls, and taking on a more domestic role.

As you grow, those expectations shift and become more encompassing. When you start school, your parents expect you to do well. Most children grow up with the expectation that they'll go on to attend university or college and start in a good, well-paying career.

Whatever the expectations, they're always there, and they are rarely outwardly stated. Your parents and family members might not say that they expect certain things from you, but those expectations are implicit.

While you're certainly not forced to meet those expectations, the threat of disappointing those closest to you can be an awful motivator. In the worst-case scenario, you could end up living to please the expectations of others due to fear of disappointment and rejection.

Overall, how do you know if you're living according to the expectations of others, rather than living for yourself?

One of the key indicators that you might be being stifled under the expectations of others is being dissatisfied and frustrated with your life. It is characterized by feelings of anger, feeling unfulfilled, and sometimes resenting others who are pursuing their dreams (Klyus, 2020).

If any of this sounds familiar, I want you to take a moment to ask yourself, "Am I living the life I truly want to live?" and "Is this what I have envisioned for my life?" If the answer to both of these questions are no, then think about why.

Is the disconnect due to your own expectations or because of the expectations of others?

If the disconnect is caused by the expectations of others, I would advise that you truly think about what you want out of life and whether you're happy living your life for other people.

One client, a professional basketball player, was struggling, and as we worked through the system, we uncovered the fact that he was trying to live up to the expectations of others.

He was listening to what others were saying. Things like, *If you shot more, you'd be more of a threat.*

But, these expectations were unrealistic to him because it wasn't what he wanted. Trying to live up to the expectations of others left him drained and feeling a sense of failure.

Over the next six weeks, he realized the power of living up to his values and expectations. We uncovered his three core values (more on those later) and worked out how to play in a way that was more in line with them. When we got this right, he told me he was playing with a freedom he'd not experienced in years.

He told me his mental health was 100% better.

If you're ready to move out from under the weight of others' expectations, here are a few ways that you can handle those expectations without losing yourself to them.

Be Assertive

One of the best ways to manage the expectations of others is to be assertive about your own needs and wants ("Managing people's expectations of you," 2020).

The difficulty with being assertive is that those closest to you might not respect your wishes and find offense once you refuse to do what they want you to do. It then becomes quite tricky to navigate their expectations without causing damage to the relationship.

However, in cases where the people in your life are crushing you under the weight of their expectations, it is best to dig your heels into the sand and stand your ground. Do not budge.

After all, your life is your own. It belongs to you and no one else. You decide how to live and what to do with your life.

Set Firm Boundaries

In addition to being assertive, you need to set firm boundaries for the people in your life, particularly those who tend to be overbearing.

These boundaries can be anything that helps you live your best life and keeps external expectations at bay. For example, a boundary that you might have is that your family members aren't allowed to comment on your job or offer unsolicited advice or comments on your life.

A good boundary could also be telling close family members that they are not allowed to interfere with your personal or professional life.

By setting boundaries, you're not just asserting your own rules on how you want to live your life, but you're also letting close family members know that you won't be held to their expectations.

Accept That You Aren't in Control of the Expectations Others Have of You

While you can control how you respond to the expectations of others, you cannot control the kind of expectations that others have of you or the way they choose to express it.

You also cannot control whether people respect your boundaries.

Not everyone is as open to shifting their expectations or perspectives, and there isn't much you can do about it. This might mean that you'll have to rethink your relationships with people who refuse to accept your boundaries.

While this can be quite a difficult pill to swallow, realizing that you cannot control others can also be quite freeing.

The Actress and I

Amelia spoke to the person on the other end of the phone. Her best friend never rejected her calls, and to an outsider, they seemed to be inseparable.

However, while they were friends, it was more complicated than that. They had grown close over the years, and Amelia was used to driving her friend everywhere, including auditions. Amelia's friend held the spotlight.

These experiences of always being in her shadow had caused Amelia to develop the expectation that she would always be second-best to her friend. She expected that her friend would always get the best roles even if they both auditioned for it.

This expectation has caused Amelia to begin self-sabotaging. Since she expected that she'd be second-best, she would deliver subpar performances in auditions. It was a self-fulfilling prophecy.

After this phone call, their relationship would change forever. Amelia was finally ready to be honest with herself and with her best friend.

Coaching Action

This coaching action is quite similar to the one outlined in "Chapter 3: Self-Talk." However, this time, instead of focusing on a person you look up to and who brings positivity to your life, we'll be focusing on someone who brings negativity into your life.

When I think about someone who brings negativity into my life, I am forced to reconnect with my past. I am no longer the person who lets people with negative energy into my life, nor do I allow them to creep in.

I am able to stay away from people with negative energy because I've been able to stay aligned with my core values and manage my thoughts.

Thinking about the person—or people—that have had a negative impact on your life can be quite upsetting. Getting over those feelings of frustration and anger that they inspire can be difficult.

Even now, after all these years, if I think about a specific person, many bad words come to mind, and I feel myself getting sick.

The negative thoughts and feelings that thinking about that person brings up is not healthy and can affect how you feel and act.

For this exercise, I want you to turn off your phone and remove yourself from distractions.

Think about someone who has brought negativity into your life. What words and images come to mind. How does this person make you feel? Are they still in your life? If so, why?

Think about their impact on your life and how this negativity has affected your actions.

The aim with this exercise is to become more aware of how negativity affects your life and how it makes you feel and act.

Chapter 5:

Relationships

*H*ave you ever heard the saying, "No man is an island"? Well, truer words have yet to be spoken. It is impossible to go through life being completely disconnected from others.

This might sound like a gross generalization, but think about it: Everything in our lives requires other people. If we want to make some breakfast, chances are you bought our cereal from a store. Someone packaged that cereal, a group of people made the cereal, and a cashier rang you up.

Every part of the process involved people.

When we're born, we're raised by other people. Our families play a huge role in our early development, and later on, we're introduced to friends, classmates, and colleagues.

The introduction of social media has added even more people to our lives, and in this day and age, we're more connected than ever before.

All these relationships and social connections have a huge effect on our lives, our perceptions, and our general well-being.

This chapter aims to raise your awareness of how relationships and social connections impact your perceptions and thinking. It can also impact the way you see yourself and others.

In this chapter, I'll be discussing relationships in general since many of the key features of healthy and unhealthy relationships overlap between different kinds of relationships. For example, respect and clear communication is something that every kind of relationship should have.

Instead, I'll be splitting relationships up into positive and negative (toxic) relationships. I'll also be discussing the importance of setting boundaries and going into healthy and unhealthy boundaries.

Lastly, I end with a coaching action that is focused on observing without passing judgement.

The Influence Others Have on Your Perceptions

Most people have an inner circle, whether they're aware of it or not. Your inner circle consists of the people that you're closest to. This could be your close friends, perhaps family members, and sometimes it could be friends that you've met online.

Either way, in my experience your inner circle and the people you choose to surround yourself with has the largest impact on your life. Their influence on your life is often subtle and can happen without you noticing.

For example, you could be really into a certain kind of music, and your friend might prefer a different kind of music. After spending a lot of time together, you might notice that your taste in music begins to shift, and slowly, you adopt your friend's taste.

This influence can extend to your perceptions of the world and can change how you think or your opinions on certain things. I remember going to one of my first basketball camps and being surrounded by people with backgrounds vastly different from mine.

I remember sharing accommodation and being constantly surrounded by different kinds of people—that experience changed me. Being exposed to different worldviews, perspectives, and then having conversations with people who thought differently than I did changed the way I saw the world.

I became more open minded. I tried my hardest to understand others' perspectives instead of judging them. I realized that just because someone's opinion was different than mine didn't mean that it was any less valid.

Without realizing it, the people around me influenced my perspectives and my way of thinking. In many ways, I am a mosaic of the people I've surrounded myself with, and I've become a better person for it.

However, as much as people can have a positive impact and influence on you, they can also have a negative impact on you.

In the previous chapter, I led you through an exercise where I had you think about someone negative in your life. I wanted you to think about the impact on your life, and now, I want you to think about the possible influences they might have had on you.

How have your perspectives changed since they entered your life? Now, it might be hard to admit that their negative energy might've rubbed off on you, but you have nothing to be afraid of. Having negative traits doesn't necessarily make you a negative, toxic person.

Negative emotions and energy often have a greater impact on our lives than positive ones, and getting rid of the negative influences this has on us is quite hard. Being around negative people can make us think more negatively and view the world as being a cup half empty instead of half full.

While you can unlearn these negative habits, it can be difficult.

The point here is that the people you surround yourself with directly influence your perspective of the world, of yourself, and of the people around you. If you surround yourself with negative people, you'll become a negative person. If you surround yourself with positive people, you'll become a positive person.

Positive Relationships

People are pack animals. We have an inherent need to be close to other people. We have an innate desire to connect and build meaningful relationships with others. Our need for company is almost compulsive (Northwestern Medicine Staff, 2017).

Given the level of influence our inner circle has on our development, perspectives, and well-being, it is better to fulfill our need for companionship with positive relationships instead of negative relationships.

Healthy, positive relationships are vital to our well-being and development. As I've mentioned, we're constantly surrounded by people and influenced by them. Positive influences are more likely to enrich our lives than negative ones.

A positive relationship can occur between any two people—or group of people—who love, support, and respect each other. They are also able to offer emotional support.

Key Characteristics and Benefits of Positive Relationships

Positive relationships, regardless of whether they occur between family members, partners, or friends, share certain characteristics. Being aware of these characteristics is a great way to evaluate your relationships and determine whether they are healthy or not.

Key characteristics of positive relationships include treating each other with mutual respect and kindness; being able to trust each other fully; and having an open, honest line of communication.

Open, honest—and more importantly—effective communication is one of the most important aspects of any relationship. Being able to effectively communicate with someone allows you to communicate your boundaries, your emotions, and your perspectives. It allows the relationship to grow and develop in a manner that suits both parties without causing any resentment or ill feelings.

Communication is also a great way to ensure that a positive relationship doesn't go sour.

A positive relationship can also act as a safe space where you are able to express your thoughts and feelings without the fear of being judged ("Positive relationships," 2018).

A huge factor within positive relationships is empathy. Being able to listen to and understand each other is important for any relationship.

Being able to experience and be surrounded by positive relationships has major benefits on our development and well-being. These benefits include:

Experiencing Less Stress

Being in a healthy relationship or being part of a healthy relationship, whether familial or social, has been shown to reduce stress. It has also been shown that people in healthy relationships are less responsive to psychological stress since they receive emotional and social support within their relationships (Northwestern Medicine Staff, 2017).

When I joined a basketball team, I was around people with a common interest, and my world revolved around basketball activities. I was playing all the time.

This kind of lifestyle was challenging due to the expectations that others put on me but also the expectations I put on myself. However, one of the things that gave me an escape from the stress and pressure was the relationships I forged with teammates. We developed healthy, close relationships, and although we all had very different lives, we were able to support each other in our times of need.

Having that support within the team made my time at university truly memorable and helped me achieve my goals.

Healthier Behaviors

Given that the people around us influence us, it is no surprise that healthier behaviors are a given in healthy relationships—this might be both tangible and intangible behaviors (Northwestern Medicine Staff, 2017).

For example, your partner, friend, or family member might encourage you to give up some bad habits such as smoking or eating large amounts of junk food (Northwestern Medicine Staff, 2017). These relationships could also include helping you work through negative thoughts and begin to practice things like positive self-talk.

After all, people in healthy relationships want what's best for each other and they push each other to be the best version of themselves.

Having a Greater Sense of Purpose

It is human nature to want to be needed and to feel as though we're part of something greater than ourselves. We want to belong.

Being in a loving, healthy relationship, whether that is being part of a family that is warm and welcoming or belonging to a friendship group that is accepting, can give one a sense of purpose. It can give us a sense that we have a place in the world and that we aren't lost.

This feeling can encourage us to do better, whether that is offering support to the people in our social groups or simply trying to be better than we were before. Having this sense of purpose gives our lives meaning.

While we can find meaning in other aspects of our lives, such as our work or hobbies, these activities still include people.

For example, having a healthy relationship with your colleagues greatly increases your enjoyment of your work.

Helps You Become a Better Version of Yourself

Being surrounded by people who value you and accept you for who you are is an amazing feeling. There is a freedom in being able to express your true feelings and personality without fear of being rejected or judged (Becker-Phelps, 2020).

Being in this kind of environment can help you become the ideal version of yourself—it can influence you to be a better person. It gives you the opportunity to be a more caring, open person.

After all, if you are being treated well by others, it is only natural for you to want to treat others well.

Negative (Toxic) Relationships

On the flip side of the coin, negative relationships offer none of the benefits of positive relationships, nor do they share any characteristics. Negative relationships are the antithesis of positive relationships and exist on the opposite side of the spectrum.

Negative relationships can be defined as relationships that lack respect and support. Instead, the participants of that relationship seek to undermine each other (Ducharme, 2018). There is also a distinct lack of social cohesion.

While most relationships, even positive ones, have their ups and downs, negative relationships are consistently draining and unpleasant. The negative aspects of the relationship far outweigh the positive aspects.

These kinds of relationships are notorious for being mentally and emotionally damaging to its participants (Ducharme, 2018). In worst-case scenarios, it can also be physically damaging.

Characteristics of Negative Relationships

Knowing the key characteristics of negative relationships is the first step to being able to identify whether a relationship is good for you or not. Now, it is normal for you to experience ups and downs in your relationships with others. People have different perspectives and opinions and might not always get along.

However, negative relationships go far beyond that. The biggest characteristic of a negative relationship is having to constantly sacrifice your own needs in lieu of the wants and needs of others.

In addition to having to sacrifice your own needs and wants, you might also be made to feel as though you have to forfeit your own voice, your opinions, and your wishes (Regan, 2020). Oftentimes, your needs and wants are overtaken by the needs and wants of the other participants of the relationship.

Another key characteristic is that spending time with the people in this relationship could leave you feeling emotionally and mentally drained. These kinds of relationships can also make you feel unsafe, particularly if the relationship contains emotional, psychological, or physical abuse (Regan, 2020).

Another characteristic is that the other person, or people, in the relationship might try to gaslight you. What this means is that they will try to deny your feelings and your reality and make you doubt the validity of your feelings.

As I've said before, the key to a positive, healthy relationship is communication. In negative relationships, communication isn't a factor. The communication is minimal at most, and even if it does occur, it is not effective. The participants in that relationship don't empathize or understand each other.

The constant strain of being in a negative relationship could also cause the participants in the relationship to begin resenting each other. These kinds of relationships can bring out the worst in people, and being surrounded by that kind of negative energy can have a huge impact on your well-being.

What to Do if You're in a Negative Relationship

Whenever I'm confronted with a client who is stuck in a negative relationship, my gut instinct is always to tell them to leave.

Run! I want to scream, "Run away, and don't look back!"

However, running away and cutting that person from your life isn't as simple as that. Sometimes, you don't want to lose the relationship. It can be extremely difficult, or even dangerous, to leave.

That being said, the first thing you should do if you realize that you're in a negative relationship is to decide whether the relationship is worth saving or not. Ask yourself whether you want to stay or not.

If you want to stay in that relationship and keep the other person in your life, is it possible to fix the relationship? Is it possible to change the relationship from negative to positive?

The answer to this question is simple, the relationship is salvageable if both you and the other person are willing to make actionable changes. This includes admitting your roles in the negativity of the relationship, admitting your own faults and flaws, and trying to fix your negative behaviors.

However, if you decide to try and fix the relationship, you need to make peace with the fact that the other person might not want to change. They might not want to put in the work to improve the relationship, or they might simply not recognize their behaviors as being toxic.

You need to ultimately come to terms with the fact that you can't change people or control their actions.

Sometimes it is best to just walk away, especially if the relationship has become abusive.

I married in my mid-twenties. My wife had a daughter from a previous relationship, and I filled the stepfather role the best I could. Though I enjoyed that part of the relationship, it was the struggles with my wife that finally led me to make the choice to leave.

We talked about changing and doing things differently, but I had lost the sense of who I was and my purpose. I'd lost friends and stopped doing the things I enjoyed, like playing basketball. I remember the moment I chose to leave. If you're reading this and thinking why I left a woman and her daughter alone, let me tell you—she wasn't alone, if you know what I mean.

I had to rediscover who I was and reconnect with the people that mattered in my life; once I made that choice, the feeling of freedom I experienced was overwhelming in a positive way.

I was back!

Setting Boundaries

In the previous chapter, I briefly discussed boundaries and their importance in managing others' expectations. However, what exactly are boundaries, and how do you set them?

Boundaries, by definition, refer to a limit of something or a line that marks the edge of something. When applied to relationships, a boundary is a guideline that you can create in order to let people know how to behave around you (Hutchinson, 2018). It also lets them know what you're willing to put up with and the kind of behavior that you're adverse to.

Setting boundaries within a relationship, whether familial, work related, or romantic, is important because it ensures that the relationship remains mutually respectful, caring, and appropriate (Hutchinson, 2018). It also ensures that the needs and wants of both parties are met.

Setting boundaries sounds simple, right? It seems mutually beneficial for everyone involved. "You respect me and I'll respect you," right?

Not quite.

It's easy to assume that people will respect our boundaries, however, this might not always be the case. Remember, we're all raised differently, and we all have different morals and values.

What might be socially acceptable to you might not be socially acceptable to others. Cultural and societal norms differ, and often, this difference is reflected in the kinds of boundaries people set.

Therefore, someone might not understand why you have certain boundaries, and you might not understand why others have certain boundaries. For example, someone might have a boundary that requires others to never comment on their physical appearance, even if it's to compliment it. You might find that strange if complimenting and commenting on someone's physical appearance is something that is commonplace in your upbringing and social circle.

No matter the differences, or whether you understand it or not, the key is to respect other people's boundaries as you'd want your own to be respected.

There are two main kinds of boundaries: physical boundaries and emotional boundaries. Physical boundaries are most common and include your body, your personal space, and privacy (Camins, 2016). It could also include your belongings, your home, and extend to pets.

Violations of your physical boundaries could include standing too close to you, people touching you, or people going through your things without your permission.

Emotional boundaries are characterized by separating your feelings from the feelings of others (Camins, 2016). Violating these boundaries include letting the feelings of others dictate your own, taking responsibility for others' feelings, or sacrificing your own needs to please others.

Having boundaries is also a way of protecting your self-esteem and your identity as an individual. They also help to protect yourself and your physical and emotional spaces from unwanted intrusion (Soghomonian, 2019).

In my experience, I find that setting boundaries can be quite empowering. It allows me to make healthy decisions for my own life, and it allows me to take responsibility for myself.

Here are a few tips on how to set effective boundaries:

Understand and Value Your Needs

Up until now, you might have been avoiding setting boundaries because you were afraid of offending or hurting the people in your life. You could have also avoided setting boundaries because you were unable to clearly define your needs and wants.

Therefore, before you set your boundaries, I would advise that you clearly define your needs, wants, and values. Decide what is important to you and how you'd like others to treat you.

You also need to realize that your needs, wants, and values are important and deserve to be respected. You deserve to be respected.

Have Realistic Expectations

We've had an entire chapter dedicated to expectations and on the importance of managing your expectations. The lessons learned there apply here as well.

You need to make peace with the fact that not everyone is going to respect your boundaries (Soghomonian, 2019). In fact, when setting boundaries, you might cause conflict.

For example, you might have family members that don't understand the boundaries you've set, either because they don't want to or because they don't respect you. You might also have people purposefully violate your boundaries as a way to disrespect you.

Therefore, I would advise that you think carefully about the social activities you participate in, especially if there are people around that are known for violating your boundaries.

Be Kind

Setting boundaries doesn't mean that you have to be abrasive to others, however, it also doesn't mean that you have to be a pushover either. Finding a balance between being firm and assertive, while remaining kind and understanding, can be a huge challenge.

However, explaining your boundaries with kindness and empathy goes a long way toward having people accept and respect them (Soghomonian, 2019). This is especially effective with difficult family members, partners, or colleagues.

Be Assertive

When you're first setting boundaries, you might experience some pushback from people who have become accustomed to treating you in a certain way. Whether it's a gossipy aunt who likes to make snide comments about your body and lifestyle or a cousin always crosses the line when teasing you, there are going to be people who are going to push your boundaries as much as they can.

In cases like this, being assertive and standing your ground can be enough to get those people to back off. Don't be afraid to stand up for yourself.

Don't Be Afraid to Walk Away

Sometimes, no matter how assertive and respectful you are, some people are going to refuse to respect you and the boundaries you set. In cases like this, it might be best for you to just get up and walk away.

You have the option of leaving the situation and limiting the amount of time you spend with that person (Soghomonian, 2019). There is no point in arguing with people who refuse to listen and understand you. Remember, you can't control their actions, but you can control yours.

Sometimes, trying to reason with people just isn't worth the time or effort.

The Actress and I

In our sessions, Amelia revealed more about her relationship with her friend, and we delved deeper into the inner workings of their friendship.

During a particularly emotional session, Amelia revealed that she often felt emotionally and mentally drained after spending extended periods of time with her friend. Their relationship was characterized by Amelia constantly pushing her feelings, needs, and wants aside in order to accommodate her friend.

She often went above and beyond to ensure that her friend felt safe, loved, and understood. However, these considerations and efforts were rarely extended toward Amelia.

Amelia had long pushed her feelings aside because she feared offending her friend; however, those apprehensions were long gone.

Amelia now realizes that she deserves to be respected and has decided to set some boundaries.

Now, as she cradles the phone to her ear, I believe that she's finally ready to take the next step and change their friendship dynamic for the better.

Coaching Action: Awareness Without Judgment

Up until this point, the coaching exercises have involved you connecting with your physical self, expanding your awareness to your thoughts and to the world around you.

I have also guided you through experiencing both positive and negative emotions by thinking about someone positive in your life and someone negative in your life. By using these exercises, you've been able to recognize the effects these relationships have had on you and how they've made you feel.

Now, we're going to take a step further and observe without passing judgment.

Observing without judgment is said to be one of the highest forms of intelligence. A practitioner who is able to observe without passing judgment is said to experience true inner peace.

This practice involves removing your emotions from a situation, be it negative or positive, and simply observe. When you look at certain things in our environment, for example, you might think that it looks like or that you need to tidy up because it's slightly messy. In doing so, you are both observing and passing judgment based on your beliefs of how things should be.

For this exercise, I want you to switch off your phone and remove yourself from distractions. I want you to observe your environment without passing judgments, statements, or criticism.

Simply observe and accept.

Begin by looking at an object and say to yourself, "This is a [x]." Then, end your thought. Don't judge; don't compare. Just accept.

The aim of this exercise is to help you learn to accept things for what they are without passing judgment. When we remove judgment and accept the things we cannot change, our levels of anxiety and stress are greatly reduced.

Chapter 6:

Shut Up! The Thought Recipe

*E*very second of every day, we're bombarded with millions of bits of information that are constantly being processed, evaluated, and filed away. All of this occurs without us being aware of it.

Right now, you're reading the words on this page and actively, consciously processing the information. At the same time, you could be feeling the wind on your skin or the light from a nearby lamp. You're also processing any background noises and activity. What I find so fascinating is that your brain is able to process and absorb all of this information while you remain engrossed by this book.

What interests me most is what the brain chooses to focus on and remember. For example, if you're taking a test, you might be unable to remember the contents of what you studied but the entire soundtrack of *Hamilton* might be running loops through your mind.

Why does this happen? Why can I still remember silly details from my childhood when I can't remember what I had for breakfast yesterday?

The concept of thoughts and the way our brains process information is fascinating to me.

This chapter expands on our discussion on submodalities in "Chapter 3: Self-Talk" and hopefully expands your understanding of how your thoughts and perceptions occur and how they affect your actions.

This is done with the aim of helping you understand that you are fully in control of your thoughts and perceptions and have power over them.

In this chapter, I'll discuss the concept of the thought recipe and how the thought recipe would work in practice. Lastly, we end off with a coaching action that urges you to regularly practice the thought recipe.

The Thought Recipe

What is the thought recipe and why is it so important?

Well, think about an actual recipe. Perhaps a recipe for donuts. In order to make the donuts, you need to gather the proper ingredients such as flour, eggs, sugar, and whatever else.

Once you have the ingredients, you follow the recipe and boom! You've got donuts!

I might have skipped a couple of steps, but you get my point.

A thought recipe is based on this concept. It follows the same core principles but instead of flour and eggs as your ingredients, you'll have visual, audio, and kinesthetic communication systems.

These submodalities are what our thoughts and actions are made up of, but instead of the aim being a lovely batch of donuts, the aim of the thought recipe is to be happy and improve your life and well-being.

However, right now, the thought recipe you're using isn't resulting in happiness or satisfaction. Something in the recipe is wrong.

Now, if you're making donuts and they turn out tasting funny or looking strange, you chuck them out and try again by tweaking the recipe. The same concept applies here. If the thought recipe isn't working, change the recipe.

The theory behind this concept is quite simple. Change the thought: Change the outcome.

As mentioned, there are three main ingredients to thinking. These are visual, auditory, and kinesthetic, both internally and externally.

The visual aspect represents what and how you see the external world as well as what you see internally with your mind's eye. The auditory aspect represents how and what you hear in the world around you as well as your internal self-talk. Lastly, the kinesthetic aspect represents how you act and behave as well as what you feel (your emotions).

The combination of these submodalities creates thoughts, and in turn, these thoughts affect your actions and perspectives. Therefore, submodalities are the ways in which you think.

For example, when we think about the concept of self-talk, the submodalities attached to this concept could be how loud the voice is, who the voice sounds like, and the tone of voice.

The core idea here is that the more submodalities we're able to identify within a thought, the better our chances of changing a potential negative thought to a positive one. Your thoughts and the submodalities attached to it creates your recipe.

It could be said that your mind uses these recipes to interpret the world around you with the visual, auditory, and kinesthetic acting as ingredients to the recipe. Following this thinking, the way that you interpret information is the method the recipe uses.

It is then believed that if your recipe isn't correct, you'll experience more internal struggles. On the flip side, if your recipe is correct, you'll flourish.

The Thought Recipe in Practice

Now that you have an idea about what the thought recipe is and what it entails, let's put this concept into practice.

By practicing a thought recipe, it is believed that you would be able to control your thoughts and your actions. When using this method, what you want to aim for is the ability to recognize wasteful, negative, or unproductive thoughts before you inevitably act on them.

For example, say you're in the supermarket, grabbing a few things for dinner. You've had a long, stressful day at work, and the only thing keeping you going is the thought of going home and having a hot bath.

You're walking down one of the aisles when someone harshly bumps into you, causing you to drop something. The person doesn't stop to say sorry but simply walks off as if nothing ever happened. Your first thought might be to yell at them and say something mean.

Oftentimes, when we're overly tired and stressed out, our verbal filter switches off. So ultimately, the time between you thinking of yelling at the person and then following through with the action might be very short.

However, if you've been practicing the thought recipe, you might pause and recognize that the thought you had was both negative and unproductive. You might then change your thinking.

Instead of having the perception that the person who bumped into you is rude and inconsiderate, you might consider that just like you, they're having a bad day and didn't mean to bump into you. Your thinking could then shift from being negative to being contemplative.

This would then change your action. Instead of yelling at the person, you show some kindness and let it go.

This is an example of how practicing the thought recipe could change your actions and perceptions. However, in what way does one practice a thought recipe? How does it work?

First, I want you to find a quiet, peaceful place and think about the behaviors that you display that you'd like to change. Ask yourself if you simply want to begin taking action in order to do the things you keep telling yourself to do. Are you plagued with negative self-talk and want to shift this to positive self-talk?

Once you've identified the behaviors you want to change, I want you to try reverse engineering the process of how your behavior came to be. By now, you know that your behavior is influenced by your emotions, which are influenced by your thoughts.

Within the context of this book, those thoughts would be your negative self-talk.

Next, think about the behavior you want to change and then think about the emotion behind that behavior. What are you feeling when you act like that?

Once you've identified the emotion attached to that behavior, think about which negative self-talk caused this emotion. What are you saying to make yourself feel this way?

Now that you have those words in your mind, think about which words you can replace in order to turn that negative self-talk into positive self-talk. For example, *can't* ends up as *can*, *won't* is then *will*, and *why* becomes *when*.

Here's a scenario: You are a chronic procrastinator. For some reason, you always wait until the last moment to complete your tasks at work. Lately, that behavior has had a negative impact on your work performance and overall work ethic.

You've been missing deadlines, and your boss has started to comment on your poor performance. However, no matter how much effort you put in, you can't help but procrastinate day in and day out.

In this case, a thought recipe practice might help you change this kind of behavior.

By doing the thought recipe practice, you realize that your procrastination stems from feelings of the fear of failure, and that these emotions come from negative self-talk that says, "You'll never be good enough to succeed so why even try?" and ruins your outlook.

You could then change that negative self-talk to positive self-talk by changing a few words. Instead of thinking, *You'll never be good enough*, think, *You are enough*. Then, you could change, *So why even try?* to *Try your best to succeed*.

Your negative self-talk of, *You'll never be good enough to succeed, so why even try?* then becomes positive self-talk that says, *You are enough; try your best to succeed*. To take this to another level, you can change it further and say to yourself, "You are enough, DO your best to succeed." The word "do" has a stronger intent than "try."

In addition to changing the words, I would also advise you to change the submodalities. In this case, it could be the volume and tone of your self-talk. Your negative self-talk might be a loud voice screaming at you or even speaking to you with contempt. You could concentrate on making the positive self-talk sound softer and kinder.

You could also make your positive self-talk sound like someone you look up to or admire.

By removing our negative self-talk and replacing it with positive self-talk, you can shift your energy and create a new, positive emotion to associate to that thought and change your behavior.

The Actress and I

In one of our first sessions, while Amelia was expressing her intense frustration at her inability to give her all during auditions, I suggested we try a thought recipe practice. Like many of my first-time clients, she was confused and had never heard of a thought recipe practice before.

Amelia loved cooking, so I explained the concept to her using the same donut analogy I used in the previous section.

Slowly, we worked through regressing her behavior of halfheartedly completing auditions.

I asked her to think about her last audition and the last time she displayed that behavior.

"What did you feel at that moment?" I asked her. "What emotions does that behavior bring up now?"

Amelia thought long and hard about my questions before she finally said, "Fear and insecurity."

Once she was able to identify the emotions behind her behavior, I told her to think about the thoughts she could be having that made her feel this way.

She mentioned not wanting to outshine her friend and thinking that she would never be as good of an actress as her friend.

Right there, we reached the core of her troubles. Her own thoughts were limiting her growth, and she would need to work through those negative thoughts in order to make room for positive thoughts.

After that, I handed her a notebook and told her to practice her thought recipe at least once a day, and she did. After a few weeks, she proudly rushed into my office, notebook in hand, to show me her progress. On that day, she told me she was ready to make a change.

Without changing her thought process and perspective, Amelia would've never been able to walk into my office, pick up the phone, and call her friend.

Coaching Action: Awareness of Controlling Your Thoughts

A thought recipe is a unique method in a sense that it helps you accept the fact that you can control your own thoughts. This thought recipe, like any other recipe, takes time to master. The more you practice, the better you become.

Controlling your thoughts and understanding the reasons behind them is a great way to begin managing feelings of stress, anxiety, and negative thinking. This also allows you to make room for positive thinking and begin living a more positive life.

For this exercise, I want you to turn off your phone and remove yourself from distractions. Pick up a journal or notebook, and begin listing all the behaviors that you want to change.

Next, rank them according to importance. Which behavior do you want to change first?

Write down this behavior on a fresh page and think about the emotions you feel when you act in this way. Are they negative or positive? List the emotions that come to mind.

Next, I want you to think about which thoughts make you feel these emotions. Much like with the actress, I want you to challenge the negative self-talk with positive self-talk. Change the submodalities, such as tone, volume, and even who you hear speaking, until you've changed the negative voice into a positive, motivating voice.

Continue to practice the thought recipe until your behavior has changed.

This exercise builds on the previous fundamentals you've learned. Now that you have a good foundation, you can learn to control your thoughts and manage negative self-talk.

Chapter 7:

Taking Action

*W*e've been together for a bit of time now. You've spent your precious time reading my words and—hopefully—participating in the coaching exercises.

We've spoken at great length about the impact our inner voice has on our perceptions and how the people and the world around us influences our inner voice.

So, now what? We're near the end of the book. You might be questioning what more there could possibly be to talk about. What more is there to learn?

The short answer to those questions is: everything.

This book is just the tip of the iceberg. There is so much knowledge in the world. Countless methods of practicing self-care and of living meaningfully. There are so many ways to be present.

Overall, as we near the end of this book, I urge you to take action.

I urge you to use the knowledge that you've gained by reading this book and begin actively implementing change into your life. Whether that's practicing mindfulness or learning how to manage your expectations, as long as you're doing something to improve yourself, then it is a step in the right direction.

You picked this book for a reason. You've stayed this long for a reason. Don't let your efforts be in vain.

This chapter aims to help you take action by providing you with a few tips on how to naturally implement change in your life. We then end off with our last coaching action which focuses on self-talk and its relation to your key values.

Knowledge Is Meaningless Without Action

The above statement deserves repeating: Knowledge is meaningless without action. You can be the most intelligent, well-read person around and that knowledge is completely useless if you don't do anything with it.

I'm not saying that learning for learning's sake is a bad thing. What I mean is that if you seek to learn something for a specific purpose and assume that the knowledge alone will dramatically change your life, it won't.

Knowledge is just knowledge. It exists apart from us and will continue to exist long after we're gone. I like to think of knowledge as a tool. Like any tool, it won't accomplish anything until you make use of it.

For example, if you want to begin gardening, you'll go to the store or a nursery and purchase all the tools you need and maybe even a few saplings. However, this alone won't result in a garden. All you've done is equip yourself with the tools that allow you to garden.

Knowledge functions the same way: It is merely a tool. The impact it has on your life depends on how you use it.

You cannot invoke meaningful change without knowledge; however, knowledge on its own does not result in change.

Let's take a breather for a moment. I want you to ask yourself these two questions: Do you want change? Do you want your life to change?

If the answer is yes, and I suspect it is, then you need to take action. Taking action is a basic requirement, and you can't move forward without it.

The Benefits of Taking Action

We understand that taking action leads to change. That's great and all but you might be thinking, *What else does it do?*

Sure, evoking change is great, but what other benefits does taking action offer? How will actively participating in your life improve your life?

With that being said, here are some additional benefits to taking action.

Improved Well-Being

One of the biggest benefits to taking action and having an active role in your own life is that you can begin addressing any mental, physical, or emotional distresses.

This could be as simple as beginning to actively work on improving your physical health by visiting the gym or working out at home; it could be practicing self-care or mindful meditation.

Whatever it is, being able to actively work toward improving it is a major step forward. Sometimes the road to feeling better, both mentally and physically, starts with you taking that first step.

Overcoming Fear

Often in life, we allow fear to hold us back from doing the things we truly want to do. This could be the fear of failure or rejection. Either way, this fear can so easily take a hold of us and push us into a corner that we feel we might never escape.

Fear can be paralyzing.

Taking action can help you overcome this fear and move out of that corner. It is therapy by exposure. The more you exit your comfort zone and try something new—the more you put yourself out there—the less scary it becomes.

The more you're able to face your fears and come (easier it is to overcome those fears. Taking action help

Stops the Complaining

Have you ever had a friend who just wouldn't stop complaining? Every time you get together, they complain, and it is constant. Most of the time, they're complaining about the same thing over and over until it feels like you're going mad.

You think to yourself that if they're complaining this much about something, why don't they do something to change it?

That is the heart of the issue right there.

They wouldn't need to complain if they just did something about it (Mercury, 2016), and the same thing goes for you.

If you're unhappy about something in your life, don't complain about it. Do something to change it!

It really is that simple: Just take action.

Boosts Your Self-Confidence

No matter where you are in life or what position you hold, chances are that there's something in your life that requires you to take action. This could be focusing on your mental health, cleaning the pool, or cleaning out your closet. No matter the activity, the longer you procrastinate, the more you might be beating yourself up about it.

This opens up room for negative self-talk like, *Why am I so lazy?*, or *Why can't I get things done?* This negative self-talk can have a ripple effect and really affect your self-confidence.

Taking action eliminates all of this negative self-talk and allows you to experience a sense of achievement. You've done the thing! No matter how big or small the task, you did it.

instantly makes you feel more confident and capable. By consistently taking action, you are consistently proving to yourself that you are a capable person. You are proving your abilities to yourself.

Knowing that you can do something, and that you can do it well, is a great confidence booster.

Increasing Your Satisfaction and Minimizing Your Regrets

Life feels worth living when you begin to take action. You are able to go to bed each night knowing that you've accomplished something and have taken one step toward your goals.

Waking up in the morning with a sense of purpose is a great way to start the day. You know what you want, you know how to get it, and you're excited to get going.

Taking action gives you a sense of purpose. It allows you to pursue the things that you want without hesitation. You are able to satisfy your need for personal and professional growth and development.

Taking action means that nothing is strong enough to hold you back for long. It is about more than just making changes—it is about persevering in the face of adversity. Knowing that you're doing your best to achieve your goals is satisfying, especially when you begin seeing results.

In addition to leaving you satisfied, taking action minimizes any regrets you might have. After all, taking action means going after what you want, which means that you won't have to regret missing an opportunity because you were too scared to pursue it.

You might look back on your life and realize that you had the opportunity to be a part of something amazing, only you never took action. This could've been because of fear or uncertainty. Whatever it was, you froze, and the opportunity passed you by.

By actively taking action, you can minimize your feelings of regret by acting on opportunities that interest you. Even if they don't pan out, at least you'll be comforted by the knowledge that you tried.

Turning Your Dreams Into Reality

Now that we've discussed the importance and benefits of taking action, let's address how to take action.

Often, I've found that while most people want to take action and make a change, not many do. This could be for a myriad of reasons, but the most common one, in my experience, is simply because they don't know how.

You might have a goal in mind, and you might know where you're beginning, but you might not know how to reach that goal. It is the journey that you're having trouble with.

With that being said, here are a few tips to help you begin implementing change in your life:

Knowing What You Want

Now, we know that taking action is important, but sometimes, we don't know how to do it. Taking action is hard. It requires us to leave our warm comfort zone and venture out into the proverbial cold in search of *something*.

The harsh truth is that sometimes we don't know what that something is. Sometimes, all we know is that something is missing—something is off.

Therefore, the first step to making actionable changes to your life is knowing what you want. Your goals or dreams don't have to be lofty or grand in order to be worthy of attention.

Your goal could be to start getting up earlier in order to get to the gym or it could be to start learning how to cook. No matter the goal, having one offers you a road map.

It gives you something to work toward and build up to. In some ways, having goals is much like having a purpose.

Do the Most Important Thing First

This is not a revolutionary thought or action. All this tip entails is rearranging your daily to-do list and putting the most important thing, or most difficult thing, first and then doing it first (Edberg, 2021).

By doing the most difficult, time-consuming task first, you open up the rest of your day for lighter, easier tasks. This is a great method if you do all your best work in the morning (Edberg, 2021).

It also leaves your afternoons open for less time-consuming tasks and allows you to wind down after a long day.

Having the most important thing done before noon lifts a weight from your shoulders, and you continue the rest of your day feeling good about yourself.

Anything Worth Doing Is Worth Doing Poorly

Sometimes, the strain of having to take action and actively participate in our lives can be overwhelming. Some mornings, even getting out of bed can feel like having to move mountains.

On days where life has taken its toll on you, it's okay to take things easy. It's okay to take a break.

Someone once told me that anything worth doing is worth doing poorly, and at first, I didn't understand what they meant by that. After a lifetime of being told to give my all and always put in 100%, doing poorly wasn't in my vocabulary.

However, the person explained what they meant, and this tip has changed my life. They told me that doing a little bit is better than doing nothing at all.

If you're too drained to meditate for an hour, mediate for five minutes. If the thought of going to the gym is just too much, just take a walk. You might not be doing the "best," but you're doing your best.

You're showing up—sometimes, that's enough.

Don't Forget to Rest

Oftentimes, when we're working toward a goal that is particularly important to us, we tend to overwork ourselves. We push ourselves hard because it is something we really want. We might also push ourselves hard because we're afraid of failure or we're impatient. Sometimes it's just because we've overestimated ourselves and our abilities.

Overworking yourself might be a quick way to reach your goal, but it is also a quick way to hit burnout. It also means that we're not taking care of ourselves.

Being completely worn out can leave you feeling completely drained and without energy or motivation. It means that you've run out of steam and that, as much as you want to, you cannot continue.

By taking regular, effective breaks, you can diminish the overall effects of burnout as well as allow yourself to rest.

Knowing when to rest and when to take action is a balancing act that not many have figured out. I think the key is realizing that just because you're resting doesn't mean you're not taking action.

Resting is taking action toward improving your health. It is a form of self-care.

Focus On the How-To

When faced with a challenge, a new goal, or a new opportunity, instead of thinking about the end result and wondering the what-if scenario, think about the how-to scenario (Edberg, 2021). What I mean by this is that you should focus on how to tackle these challenges instead of wondering how much better your life would be if they simply didn't exist.

Focusing on the how-to allows you to figure out new ways of taking action and dealing with the challenge at hand. It also prevents you from dwelling on the negatives and thinking about everything that could go wrong (Edberg, 2021).

While it is important to consider the risks when entering new endeavors, dwelling on everything that could go wrong doesn't solve anything.

Instead of focusing on possible outcomes, focus on how to solve the problem or how to approach an opportunity. Think about what you can do instead of what might happen.

Celebrate Yourself

One of the most important things about taking action, and keeping up your motivation to take action, is taking the time to celebrate your accomplishments. Oftentimes, we forget to take stock of how far we've come and how much we've grown.

It is so easy to hyperfocus on the future and to constantly chase your dreams. However, every now and then, I'd advise you to pause and take stock. It is a good idea to look back and realize just how far you've come and how much you've achieved.

At times like this, it is a good idea to celebrate yourself. Treat yourself! Get yourself something nice!

You've worked hard, and you deserve to be treated with kindness and support.

A good way to celebrate yourself is to begin implementing little rewards for yourself each time you reach a new milestone. These rewards can be anything you want it to be, however, I would advise that you keep your rewards in line with your goals.

For example, if your goal is weight loss, don't have your reward be eating junk food or snacks. Not only is this counterproductive but it could also cause you to backslide.

The Actress and I

Amelia hung up the phone and stared at me, her eyes wide. As much as I wanted to jump up from my seat and ask her what happened, I held myself back. This was an important moment for her, and I would never want to ruin it with my impatience. She needed time to process.

She sat down and stared at her hands as though she couldn't quite believe what had just happened.

"I did it," she whispered, and then said more loudly, "I can't believe I did it!"

I looked at her, gauging her reaction "How do you feel?"

"I'm not sure."

I expected that. Her mind had yet to catch up with her actions, and I was sure she'd be replaying that conversation in her head for days to come. However, the point was that she'd finally done something. She'd finally taken action and made a change in her life and in her relationship with her friend.

"Is it bad that I feel relieved?" Amelia asked after a moment of silence.

I shook my head, "No, you've worked hard to reach this point. You have nothing to feel guilty about."

"She didn't even sound mad when I told her," she continued. "She only sounded disappointed. She wants to meet for coffee tomorrow."

"Do you want to meet her?"

"No," Amelia lifted her head, seeming more confident than she ever had before. "I told her I needed space. I told her she needed to respect that."

She smiled brightly and seemed to shake the tension from her shoulders. It was over. She'd done it! Finally, her values lined up with her behavior.

Coaching Action: Awareness of Alignment With Your Values

I want you to take a moment to think about what drives you forward. What helps you make sense of the world around you? What experiences have affected and influenced your values?

What do you value?

Do you value money or happiness? Do you value warmth or the cold? Do you value both?

These are just a few examples of some values that you might have. My core values are accountability, balance, and calm. Ever since I figured out these core values, I have lived my life according to them.

Aligning the way I lived my life to fit with my values didn't happen overnight. It took some time to get used to because before, I identified as a basketball player, and my values were completely different.

In my younger years, I valued competitiveness, winning, and fitness. These are completely different to the values I have now. Over time, you might notice that your values have changed. After all, life is in a constant flux, and we aren't the people we used to be in the past. We should be taking time to reflect and connect with the person we're growing into.

However, if we don't reevaluate our values, we could become stuck in our old ways and habits. As I aged and I was no longer able to play at the level I was used to, I had to adapt my values and expectations to meet the capabilities of my body.

Now, for this coaching action, what I want you to do is turn off your phone and remove yourself from distractions.

I want you to be conscious of your self-talk when you think about and consider your three core values. If you're experiencing any negative self-talk, it could be an indication that a part of your life isn't in line with one or more of your core values.

On the opposite end of the spectrum, if you're experiencing positive self-talk, it could be an indication that you are living your life in line with your values.

Here are a few examples of values that you might hold:

Accountability	Adventurous	Balance	Calm
Compassion	Certainty	Excitement	Fairness
Faith	Growth	Giving	Hope
Loyalty	Mindfulness	Purpose	Reliability
Stability	Teamwork	Timekeeping	Trusting

Have a look at the list and narrow them down to ten. You might have an idea of other values you're aware of, not on this list so add those. When you have your ten, narrow them down to three. This is where it can become tricky because when you hold a value, you don't want to let it go so when you feel uncertain about two, tell yourself, if you had to pick one that would really help you connect with the person you want to be, which one would it be. When you have three, reflect and try them on for size.

The aim of this exercise is to build on the idea that you know how to control your thoughts. Determine what your values are, and align your values with your self-talk.

This is the final step to mastering your self-talk.

You started this journey because you wanted to master your negative self-talk. Throughout this book you've learned new perspectives, strategies, and exercises to help you navigate and manage your inner voice.

I can only hope that you have put this theory into practice and if you want my personal help you can contact me at https://purposefulthinking.co.uk

Conclusion

*J*ust like that, we've reached the conclusion of this book. My, how time flies.

With the span of seven chapters, we've gone through a journey of learning how to master your inner voice and take control of your life. By now, you've learned all about the power of our mind and how your perceptions have the ability to play tricks on you.

You've also learned about how your environment and the people around you can influence your perceptions, thoughts, and inner self-talk. I have even gone on to discuss self-talk in great length in "Chapter 3: Self-Talk," just so that you would have a clear idea of what we were speaking about.

I then went on to address the impact internal and external expectations have on your perceptions, actions, and well-being. In that chapter, we looked at the various kinds of expectations others could have on you and ones that you could be placing on yourself. I also spoke about the importance of learning how to manage and deal with those expectations.

We then looked at the influence your relationships have on your perspectives, thoughts, and inner voice. We spoke in detail about positive and negative relationships and the effect that these kinds of relationships can have on your well-being.

I introduced you to the concept of a thought recipe and how, by practicing a thought recipe, you could shift your inner voice from negative to positive. In doing so, you'll be able to change your behavior and begin taking action.

In the final chapter, we finally discuss the importance of taking action. Without actively working toward making changes and then implementing those changes, you'll stay stuck in the same old life, doing the same thing you've always done.

In this chapter, I also gave you a few tips on how to implement change in your life in the hopes that it would give you the motivation you need to take action.

Now, this book contained more than just thoughtful discussions about how to change your life and control your inner voice. I also included the story of "The Actress and I" and coaching actions.

"The Actress and I" might have seemed like a strange thing to include. You might even have questioned the existence of Amelia and the purpose of the little stories. Whether Amelia exists or not is not the point here.

I included these stories to help you better understand the contents of the chapters by presenting them within a real-life context. Amelia's journey is meant to reflect your own.

On the other hand, the coaching actions and exercises acted as practical changes and steps that you could implement in your life in order to begin mastering your inner voice.

These exercises were placed at the end of each chapter to encourage you to use what you've learnt and put your newfound knowledge into practice.

This book has been carefully crafted to act as not only a guide but a practice guide as well. After all, knowledge is useless if you don't use it.

Key Takeaway

Taking the first step toward making a change in your life and taking action takes courage and determination. It is important to remind yourself that you've come a long way from where you started, and in that time, you've grown and changed.

In a few moments, you will put this book down and move on with your life. Before you do so, here are a few things that I would like you to remember:

- Your mind is a powerful thing. It might try to trick you or warp your perceptions but remember, you are in charge. You have complete control over your thoughts, perceptions, and actions.

- Be careful who you allow into your inner circle. People have an enormous influence on your thoughts, perceptions, and behaviors. If you want to live a more purposeful, positive life, surround yourself with positive relationships.

- Knowledge without action is useless. No matter how many self-help books you read or how many self-improvement methods you learn about, it all means nothing if you refuse to take actionable steps toward improving your life. You need to take action if you want to change your life.

- It is very possible to master your inner voice and manage negative self-talk, but it takes practice. Practice your thought recipe, and practice mindfulness.

When you first picked up this book, you held in your heart a sense of urgency and motivation. I want you to hold on to that feeling of urgency as you move past the lessons in this book.

Do not forget why you first started this journey. Constantly remind yourself of the reason why you're here. There is a reason you want to change your life, so don't allow fear to hold you back.

Like I've said, you are in control, and the power is in your hands. Go out there and take action!

The Actress and I

It has been a few weeks since I last spoke to Amelia. We had scheduled a follow-up session after her phone call to her friend, but since then, she's been flooded with auditions and life events, and the session was pushed back.

Without intending to, I tried keeping track of her progress by listening to her interviews and Instagram live streams. She seemed more confident on screen than she had the last time I'd seen her, and while that gave me hope, I remained cautious.

It would be so easy for her to pretend to be doing well behind the safety of a screen. I would only be able to tell if the exercises worked once she stepped back into my office.

After another week, Amelia bounced into my office with a huge smile on her face. Her eyes were bright and optimistic, and when I offered her a seat, she refused.

"I'm far too hyped up to sit!" she exclaimed, hopping from one foot to the other.

Before I could respond, she said, "I got it! I got the part!"

She squealed with excitement, and I couldn't help but smile. The Amelia standing in my office was a completely different person than the one I had met weeks ago. She exudes confidence and positivity. She was like a ray of sunshine.

"I am proud of you," I told her. And I meant it. She had come a long way.

She nodded, finally sitting down. "I couldn't have done it without you."

"And your relationship with your friend?"

"Better," she said. "We're still working on it, and she still slips up sometimes, but we're both really trying. We've been friends for so long; I'm glad we didn't lose that."

I understood that. Losing a friend is never easy. I sat forward in my chair feeling pretty satisfied with myself. Our time together was over. Amelia learned all she needed to from me, and I was confident that from now on, she would thrive.

"So, what's next?"

Amelia smiled as she said, "Who knows? The sky's the limit!"

Discussion Section:

Mastering Your Self-Talk for Common Experiences in Sport, Business, and Life

"Whether you think you can or whether you think you cannot, you're right" - Henry Ford (Goodreads, n.d.).

We have reached the end of our journey together, and within the next few moments, you'll close this book and move on with your life. You might take what you've learned and implement the techniques I've laid out in this book . . . or you might not.

You might even forget everything you've learned, or you might go on to pursue more knowledge and ultimately improve your life.

What I do know for sure is that I have no control over your actions—I am merely words on a page.

However, if you end up forgetting everything else, I hope you'll remember this:

- You have full control of your thoughts.

- Your thoughts lead to emotions, and those emotions lead to certain behaviors and outcomes.

- You deserve to move forward with confidence and achieve what you think you deserve.

My point is that you are in control of your life. You are responsible for your future. Whether your life changes or not is completely up to you. You decide how you react to new situations and to other people.

Before I leave you, I have one final piece of knowledge to impart.

In life, there are three experiences that are commonplace. These three experiences are breeding grounds for negative-self talk and could lead to a downward spiral. Before we end, I want to leave you with the tools to thrive when faced with these experiences.

These experiences are:

- Pressure

- Mistakes

- Losing

It can be difficult to navigate these experiences, especially if you're still struggling with mastering self-talk. Therefore, it is important to recognize these experiences for what they are and to develop healthy coping mechanisms when faced with them.

Pressure

We all experience pressures and stressors. In this day and age, it is pretty commonplace to work a high pressure job or experience stressors within your everyday life.

There are two kinds of pressures that you are likely to experience. These are internal and external pressures ("Coping Under Pressure: Survive and Thrive Under Pressure," 2019). Internal pressures are pressures that you put on yourself. This might stem from your perceived inability to meet expectations.

External pressures stem from outside sources such as perhaps your parents, teachers, or your boss. For example, you might be expected to complete a large amount of work within a short amount of time.

In extreme cases, being under large amounts of pressure can cause you to do things that go against your core values or that places your well-being at risk ("Coping Under Pressure: Survive and Thrive Under Pressure," 2019).

Pressure turns into stress when you feel that you're unable to cope with the thoughts and projected actions you might have to take. You could also think of stress as the feeling of being under too much mental and emotional pressure.

People have different ways of reacting to stress. People are also able to handle different levels of stress. For example, what might be extremely stressful for one person might be a breeze for another.

Let's look at some scenarios:

Sport

Examples of pressures that you could experience if you play a sport is that your coach might expect you to make rapid improvements to your play within a short amount of time. You might also be expected to take part in extensive practices or spend most of your time on the field or court.

Now, if you're a professional athlete this might not be an issue for you. However, if you're a student or perhaps play sports as a hobby, being expected to perform at a professional level can be quite stressful. It can also suck the fun right out of the sport you're playing.

Pressures that professional athletes could experience is needing to make key plays or constantly having to outperform themselves.

Business

Pressures that you might experience in your business or place of work could be that you need to secure clients in order to make an income. This pressure is especially prevalent if you own a small business or your main source of income is from freelance work.

Not knowing if you'll be able to pay your bills and make ends meet can be incredibly stressful and can put immense pressure on you. This can lead to feeling overwhelmed and overworking yourself as you try to do enough work to make ends meet.

Living paycheck to paycheck is stressful. It can heavily affect both your mental and physical health.

Life

The pressures you experience in life can be both internal and external. In my experience, I've found that the most prolific sources of pressure are internal.

Oftentimes, we put ourselves under immense pressure, especially if we're passionate about reaching our goals or protecting something we value. This kind of attitude isn't inherently bad. It is great to be passionate about life and about the people around you.

However, if left unchecked, this attitude could spiral into pushing yourself too far or allowing others to violate your boundaries.

For example, you might be unable to say no to certain people even if their request inconveniences you because you value that relationship. This could lead to you putting the needs of others above your own.

Dealing With Pressure

Now that we've been through the effects of pressures and where they stem from, let's discuss how to deal with it. Remember, while you might not be able to control external pressures, you can control how you react to it.

With regard to external pressures, the first tip I have for you is to try and stay organized. Try to take control of your workload by carefully organizing your day and spreading your workload out over a period of time.

Breaking down large tasks into smaller, more manageable tasks makes them much easier to tackle. It also helps to keep up your motivation.

Another tip is to schedule time to rest. In order to work and perform, you need energy. Without energy, you're not going to get things done. Therefore, I would suggest you schedule time to rest.

I would recommend trying the Pomodoro timing technique to schedule regular breaks within your workday.

The last tip I have for you is quite simple: Be kind to yourself. Realize that you are human. You are not a robot, and you don't have to constantly be pushing yourself until you burn out. You also need to manage your expectations of yourself.

You're human and you need rest. You need to be taken care of, so take care of yourself.

Mistakes

Like I said in the previous section, you're human. We're all human, and therefore, we all make mistakes. Making mistakes is as much a part of life as breathing. There really is no escaping it.

Maybe you submitted a report and later realized you forgot to add an important section, or perhaps you double-booked a client. Perhaps you called your friend by the wrong name or missed an important play during a sports match.

Either way, mistakes suck. It can make you feel ashamed and embarrassed. If the mistake occurs in the workplace, it could also damage your public image and credibility.

Let's look at a few scenarios:

Sports

If you're playing sports as a hobby or as a fun activity during a social gathering, making a mistake isn't that serious. Sure, you might be teased and feel embarrassed, but other than that, there aren't any long-lasting effects.

However, for professional athletes, making a mistake during a game can be devastating. It could be that you've missed or misunderstood an instruction from our coach or that you fumbled a catch or pass. Either way, for professional athletes, their performance on the field is vitally important.

Their sport is their job.

Business

Mistakes in business don't just result in embarrassment and other negative feelings—it could also result in losing a potential client, losing money, and harming your professional reputation.

Given that business is such a complicated field and comes with certain requirements, even the simplest mistake could be viewed as a sign of unprofessionalism.

Life

Making a mistake in life might have major repercussions or might just cause a bit of embarrassment. The consequences of that mistake depends on the scale of the mistake.

Small mistakes could be forgetting to eat breakfast or forgetting to buy some extra time at the store. These mistakes are almost inconsequential and are easily blown over.

However, large life mistakes could have sometimes devastating consequences. Mistakes like these can usually spiral into something much worse.

For example, you could make the mistake of allowing someone to violate your boundaries. While it might be fine the first or second time it occurs, it can easily become a reoccurring habit that could really affect your self-esteem, confidence, and well-being.

Dealing With Mistakes

Most mistakes are easy to deal with and don't require much effort. If you forget to buy milk, you might have to go without your morning cereal, but you're always able to get milk at a later time.

Small mistakes like these don't really have much of an impact. However, larger mistakes could need some extra intervention.

The first tip I have is to allow yourself to feel bad about your mistake. It's okay to feel bad about your mistake, especially if your mistake has had a negative impact on others. While it's okay to feel those emotions, be careful not to allow yourselves to dwell on those feelings.

The second tip I have is to keep things in perspective (Gelb, n.d.). What I mean by this is that when you make a mistake, it is easy to overinflate the impact of this mistake and blow things out of proportion. For example, you might make a typo in a business email. While you're stressing about it, your client or the recipient might not even have noticed the mistake.

The last tip I have is that if your mistake hurts someone else, apologize. If you've forgotten to pick your mom up from the airport or forgotten to attend an important event, you should apologize to the people involved and take responsibility.

Losing

We've all experienced losing. Whether we lost a race in elementary school or in a competition we entered. Chances are, we've *definitely* lost the lottery more than once. While those experiences come with feelings of disappointment, they don't have much of an effect on our lives.

After all, we can't always win. Losing is a natural part of life, and there's nothing wrong with losing. However, in some cases, losing can make us feel pretty bad about ourselves. Losing can deliver a major blow to our egos and self-esteem.

In addition to losing competitions, we could also suffer large losses such as losing someone important to us or losing our source of income. Those kinds of losses have a lasting impact on our lives, and handling that kind of loss can be quite traumatic.

Here are a few scenarios:

Sports

Once again, if you're playing sports as a hobby, then losing might not be that big of a deal. However, for professional athletes, losing a match or a tournament could mean losing sponsorships or getting removed from a sports league.

For athletes, sponsorships are an important part of their income, and losing those sponsorships could mean that they might be unable to perform or participate in future events.

This can be devastating for a professional athlete.

If you're a professional athlete on a team, such as a basketball player or soccer player, losing affects not only you but your teammates.

Business

If you run a small business, losing a client means losing a source of income. This alone can make earning a living hard. This loss can potentially have a ripple effect on your life and cause you to lose other things such as having to cut down on expenses.

You could also lose the respect of a colleague within the workplace, and while this might not directly affect your work performance, it can negatively affect your work atmosphere.

Life

Losing in life can be quite hard to handle. The most common kind of loss is losing a job or source of income. This can have pretty bad effects on your lifestyle, and in a worst-case scenario, you might not be able to pay your bills.

This alone can have tons of negative effects on your emotional and mental well-being.

Another major loss in life is the loss of a loved one. This kind of loss is especially hard to deal with since it has a major effect on our mental and emotional health. In cases where you've lost a family member or loved one, it is a good idea to surround yourself with people who support you and understand what you're going through.

It is so easy to slip into a depression and feel as though nothing will ever go right again. Climbing out of that dark place is hard, so try your hardest to prevent yourself from going down that road.

Dealing With Loss

Losing isn't great. Losing leaves you with a sense of dread and disappointment, and often, it involves having to rebuild your self-esteem. However, where there is a loss, there is always a lesson to be learned.

Most times, there is a positive takeaway from a loss. The self-talk you need to be practicing in this situation should be to ask yourself what you learned from the experience rather than dwelling on negative thoughts.

Final Thoughts

Life will throw us into the deep end as often as it can. It'll hurl us through storms as though we're nothing but rag dolls; while that isn't fun thought, it does teach us how to weather those storms.

Experiencing difficulties allows us to build our resilience. It also teaches us how to handle times of trouble.

Remember, you are in control of how you react to situations and times of difficulty. You can choose to rise to the occasion or fall.

If you enjoyed this book I'd love for you to leave a review and I'd like to invite you to find out more about me at https://purposefulthinking.co.uk

References

7 Summit Pathways. (2019). *What is Positive Self-Talk | Positive Self-Talk Quotes | 7SP.* 7 Summit Pathways. https://7summitpathways.com/blog/what-is-positive-self-talk/

Battles, M. (2016). *15 Ways to Practice Positive Self-Talk for Success.* Lifehack; Lifehack. https://www.lifehack.org/504756/self-talk-determines-your-success-15-tips

Becker-Phelps, L. (2020). *10 Benefits of Happy Relationships.* WebMD. https://blogs.webmd.com/relationships/20200715/10-benefits-of-happy-relationships

Benefits of Mindfulness. (2021). HelpGuide. https://www.helpguide.org/harvard/benefits-of-mindfulness.htm#

Bouschet, Coley. L. (2016). *How To Visually Map Out and Plan Your Future | Life Goals Mag.* Life Goals. https://lifegoalsmag.com/visually-plan-future/

Brenner, G. (2014). *10 Life-Changing Facts to Heal the Pain of the Past.* Dr. Gail Brenner. https://gailbrenner.com/2012/08/10-life-changing-facts-to-heal-the-pain-of-the-past/

Camins, S. (2016). *Setting Emotional Boundaries in Relationships.* Road to Growth Counseling; Road to Growth Counseling. https://roadtogrowthcounseling.com/importance-boundaries-relationships/

Cherry, K. (2019). *How the Fight or Flight Response Works.* Verywell Mind; Verywellmind. https://www.verywellmind.com/what-is-the-fight-or-flight-response-2795194

Chizk, G. (2019). *How To Avoid Unrealistic Expectations.* Growing Self. https://www.growingself.com/avoid-unrealistic-expectations/

Cleveland Clinic. (2019). *What Happens to Your Body During the Fight or Flight Response?* Health Essentials from Cleveland Clinic; Health Essentials from Cleveland Clinic. https://health.clevelandclinic.org/what-happens-to-your-body-during-the-fight-or-flight-response/

Coping Under Pressure: Survive and Thrive Under Pressure. (2019). Mindtools.com. https://www.mindtools.com/pages/article/coping-under-pressure.htm

Cuncic, A. (2020). *How to Stop Feeling Like an Outsider When You Have Social Anxiety.* Verywell Mind. https://www.verywellmind.com/imposter-syndrome-and-social-anxiety-disorder-4156469

Ducharme, J. (2018). *How To Tell If You're In a Toxic Relationship — And What To Do About It.* Time; Time. https://time.com/5274206/toxic-relationship-signs-help/

Edberg, H. (2021). *How to Take Action: 12 Habits that Turn Dreams into Reality.* The Positivity Blog. https://www.positivityblog.com/how-to-take-action/

Estrada, J. (2020). *6 Ways to Practice Positive Self-Talk To Improve Self Esteem.* Well+Good. https://www.wellandgood.com/positive-self-talk/

Expectation. (2021). In *Oxford Dictionary.* Lexico. https://www.lexico.com/definition/expectation

Francis, Charles. A. (2013). *How to Live in the Moment and Stop Worrying About the Future.* Lifehack. https://www.lifehack.org/articles/communication/21-instant-ways-to-live-in-the-moment.html

Gelb, S. (n.d.). *7 Steps to Take After You Make a Mistake at Work.* The Muse. https://www.themuse.com/advice/your-foolproof-guide-to-moving-on-after-you-messed-up-at-work

Gladwell, M. (2013). *Blink : the power of thinking without thinking.* Back Bay Books.

Goodreads. (n.d.). *Quote by Henry Ford.* Goodreads. https://www.goodreads.com/quotes/978-whether-you-think-you-can-or-you-think-you-can-t--you-re

Gragg, A. (2020). *Why You Should Deal with Your Past.* Decide Your Legacy. https://www.decideyourlegacy.com/why-you-should-deal-with-your-past-part-1/

Holland, K. (2018). *Positive Self-Talk: Benefits and Techniques.* Healthline. https://www.healthline.com/health/positive-self-talk#_noHeaderPrefixedContent

Hutchinson, T. (2018). *Why are Personal Boundaries Important? Your Rights in a Relationship.* Tracy Hutchinson, PhD | Fort Myers Therapy. https://www.drtracyhutchinson.com/what-are-personal-boundaries-and-why-are-they-important/

Klyus, J. (2020). *Dealing With the Pressures of Others Expectations.* Medium. https://medium.com/the-ascent/dealing-with-the-pressures-of-others-expectations-4dacfb4e3676

Laderer, A. (2020). *How to practice mindful breathing and the proven benefits that it offers.* Insider. https://www.insider.com/why-is-mindful-breathing-important

Legg, Timothy. J. (2020). *Unrealistic Expectations: 12 Examples and Tips.* Healthline. https://www.healthline.com/health/mental-health/unrealistic-expectations

Lieberman, M. D. (2003). Reflexive and reflective judgement processes: A social cognitive neuroscience approach. In *Social judgements: Implicit and explicit processes.* Cambridge University Press.

Lindberg, S. (2018). *How to Let Go: 12 Tips for Letting Go of the Past.* Healthline. https://www.healthline.com/health/how-to-let-go

Livingston, K. (2019). *NLP & Hypnosis training & education.* Hypnosis101.com. https://www.hypnosis101.com/nlp/submodalities/auditory-swish/

Managing people's expectations of you. (2020). Kids Helpline. https://kidshelpline.com.au/young-adults/issues/managing-peoples-expectations-you

Mercury. (2016, March 9). *11 Reasons Taking Action Is Crucial.* Mercury. http://www.ilanelanzen.com/personaldevelopment/11-reasons-taking-action-is-crucial/

Mindful Breathing (Greater Good in Action). (2021). Ggia.berkeley.edu. https://ggia.berkeley.edu/practice/mindful_breathing

Morris, Susan. Y. (Ed.). (2016). *What Are the Benefits of Self-Talk?* Healthline; Healthline Media. https://www.healthline.com/health/mental-health/self-talk

Northwestern Medicine Staff. (2017). *5 Benefits of Healthy Relationships.* Northwestern Medicine; https://www.nm.org/healthbeat/healthy-tips/5-benefits-of-healthy-relationships

Pappas, C. (2016, November 11). *Information Processing Basics: How The Brain Processes Information.* ELearning Industry; eLearning Industry. https://elearningindustry.com/information-processing-basics-how-brain-processes-information

Positive relationships. (2018). Dewis Wales. https://www.dewis.wales/positive-relationships-cyp

Regan, S. (2020). *19 Signs You're In A Toxic Relationship & What To Do About It.* Mindbodygreen. https://www.mindbodygreen.com/0-27419/how-toxic-relationships-affect-your-health-according-to-science.html

Saripalli, V. (2021). *Imposter Syndrome: What It Is & How to Overcome It.* Healthline. https://www.healthline.com/health/mental-health/imposter-syndrome

Schlitz, I. (2016). *How Other People Influence You and Why That's Ok.* Behavioral Scientist. https://behavioralscientist.org/invisible-influence-how-other-people-think-for-you-and-why-thats-ok/

Scott, E. (2018). *How to Reduce Negative Self-Talk for a Better Life.* Verywell Mind. https://www.verywellmind.com/negative-self-talk-and-how-it-affects-us-4161304

Scott, E. (2019). *How to Make a Plan for Lasting Life Changes.* Verywell Mind. https://www.verywellmind.com/how-to-make-a-life-plan-first-steps-3144639

Scott, E. (2020). *The Stress of Your Expectations vs. Reality.* Verywell Mind. https://www.verywellmind.com/expectation-vs-reality-trap-4570968

Social Media and Psychology | Our Wired World and Mental Health. (2019). AllPsychologySchools.com. https://www.allpsychologyschools.com/psychology/social-media-psychology/

Soghomonian, I. (2019). *Boundaries - Why are they important?* The Resilience Centre. https://www.theresiliencecentre.com.au/boundaries-why-are-they-important/

Stegner, B. (2020). *7 Negative Effects of Social Media on People and Users.* MakeUseOf. https://www.makeuseof.com/tag/negative-effects-social-media/

Submodalities. (2012). NLP World. https://www.nlpworld.co.uk/nlp-glossary/s/submodalities/

Tull, M. (2019). *The Double-Edged Sword of Childhood Trauma and Dissociation.* Verywell Mind. https://www.verywellmind.com/how-trauma-can-lead-to-dissociative-disorders-2797534

Wilding, M. J. (2017). *5 Different Types of Imposter Syndrome (and 5 Ways to Battle Each One).* Themuse.com; The Muse. https://www.themuse.com/advice/5-different-types-of-imposter-syndrome-and-5-ways-to-battle-each-one

Yang, S. (2021). *13 Steps to Take to Achieve Your Goals This Year.* TheThirty. https://thethirty.whowhatwear.com/how-to-set-realistic-expectations/slide2

Zehr, B. (2018). *Expectation vs Reality.* Intentional Impact. https://intentionalimpact.com/expectation-vs-reality/

Zeman, E. (2019). *Why It's Important to Accept Reality.* Mindsoother Therapy Center. https://www.mindsoother.com/blog/why-its-important-to-accept-reality

Printed in Great Britain
by Amazon

74525712R00078